MERCURY READER

a custom publication

Portland Community College
Essays for Reading 90

Pearson Learning Solutions

New York Boston San Francisco
London Toronto Sydney Tokyo Singapore Madrid
Mexico City Munich Paris Cape Town Hong Kong Montreal

Senior Vice President, Editorial and Marketing: Patrick F. Boles
Senior Sponsoring Editor: Natalie Danner
Development Editor: Mary Kate Paris
Assistant Editor: Jill Johnson
Operations Manager: Eric M. Kenney
Production Manager: Jennifer Berry
Rights Manager: Jillian Santos
Art Director: Renée Sartell
Cover Designers: Kristen Kiley, Blythe Russo, Tess Mattern, and Renée Sartell

Cover Art: "Gigantia Mountains & Sea of Cortes," by R.G.K. Photography, Copyright © Tony Stone Images; "Dime," courtesy of the Shaw Collection; "Open Book On Table Edge w/Pencil," courtesy of PhotoAlto Photography/Veer Incorporated; "Open Book On Table Near Table's Corner," courtesy of Fancy Photography/Veer Incorporated; "Scrabble Pieces and a Die," by G. Herbst, courtesy of PlainPicture Photography/Veer Incorporated; "Binary codes in bowls," by John Still, courtesy of Photographer's Choice/Getty Images; "Close-up of an open book," courtesy of Glowimages/Getty Images; "College Students Sitting At Tables," courtesy of Blend/PunchStock; "Red and blue circles," courtesy of Corbis Images; "Laptop screen showing photograph of landscape," courtesy of Martin Holtcamp/Getty Images; "Apples flying," courtesy of Arne Morgenstern/Getty Images.

Printed in the United States of America.

Please visit our website at *www.pearsoncustom.com.*

Attention bookstores: For permission to return any unsold stock, contact us at *pe-uscustomreturns@pearson.com.*

Pearson Learning Solutions, 501 Boylston Street, Suite 900, Boston, MA 02116
A Pearson Education Company
www.pearsoned.com

ISBN 10: 0-558-88652-3
ISBN 13: 978-0-558-88652-3

General Editors

Janice Neuleib
Illinois State University

Kathleen Shine Cain
Merrimack College

Stephen Ruffus
Salt Lake Community College

Contents

Essays on Literacy

How to Mark a Book
Mortimer Adler 1

Everything Has a Name
Helen Keller 8

Learning to Read and Write
Frederick Douglass 13

Me Talk Pretty One Day
David Sedaris 22

Mother Tongue
Amy Tan 28

What is Intelligence, Anyway?
Isaac Asimov 37

From the Poets in the Kitchen
Paule Marshall 40

Spanglish
Janice Castro and Dan Cook 52

School vs. Education
Russell Baker 56

Today's Kids Are, Like, Killing the English Language. Yeah, Right.
Kirk Johnson 60

Why My Mother Can't Speak English
Gary Engkent 66

Writing is My Passion
bell hooks 75

The Joy and Enthusiasm of Reading
Rick Moody 81

Silence
Maxine Hong Kingston 84

I Think, Therefore IM
Jennifer Lee 91

Essays on Life

Generation X
Kirsten Cole 97

We Talk, You Listen
Vine Deloria, Jr. 103

On Self-Respect
Joan Didion 114

Landscape and Narrative
Barry Lopez 120

McBastards: McDonald's and Globalization
Paul Feine 129

Building Plans: What the World Trade Center Meant
Paul Goldberger 135

The Beatles: They Changed Rock, Which Changed the Culture, Which Changed Us
Jeff Greenfield 142

The Obligation to Endure
Rachel Carson 153

I'm a Banana and Proud of It
Wayson Choy 162

Why I Want a Wife
Judy Brady 167

I Have a Dream
Martin Luther King, Jr. 172

Back to Nature
Gary Snyder 179

The Jacket
Gary Soto 183

Black Men and Public Space
Brent Staples 189

Miss U.S.A.
Studs Terkel 195

The Ethic of Compassion
The Dalai Lama 203

The Baffling Question
Bill Cosby 212

Beauty: When the Other Dancer Is the Self
Alice Walker 216

Essays on Literacy

How to Mark a Book

Mortimer Adler

Mortimer Adler (1902–2001) received his Ph.D. from Columbia University in 1928. A conservative thinker, Adler advocated education based on the "truths" found in the classical works of Western civilization. Many academic intellectuals have scorned his simple formulas for progress, but the larger culture has often embraced his ideas, as his post as chairman of the editorial board of the Encyclopedia Britannica *indicated. His Great Books project, for which he is widely known, resulted in the publication and wide circulation of handsome bound sets of important works of world literature. As you read his essay on how to mark a book, you will see a man who thought that the world is, or ought to be, clear and simple.*

1 You know you have to read "between the lines" to get the most out of anything. I want to persuade you to do something equally important in the course of your reading. I want to persuade you to "write between the lines." Unless you do, you are not likely to do the most efficient kind of reading. 1

I contend, quite bluntly, that marking up a book is not an act of mutilation but of love.

You shouldn't mark up a book which isn't yours. Librarians (or your friends) who lend you books expect you to keep them clean, and you should. If you decide that I am right about the usefulness of marking books, you will have to buy them. Most of the world's great books are available today, in reprint editions, at less than a dollar.

There are two ways in which you can own a book. The first is the property right you establish by paying for it, just as you pay for clothes and furniture. But this act of purchase is only the prelude to possession. Full ownership comes only when you have made it a part of yourself, and the best way to make yourself a part of it is by writing in it. An illustration may make the point clear. You buy a beefsteak and transfer it from the butcher's ice-box to your own. But you do not own the beefsteak in the most important sense until you consume it and get it into your bloodstream. I am arguing that books, too, must be absorbed in your bloodstream to do you any good.

Confusion about what it means to *own* a book leads people to a false reverence for paper, binding, and type—a respect for the physical thing—the craft of the printer rather than the genius of the author. They forget that it is possible for a man to acquire the idea, to possess the beauty, which a great book contains, without staking his claim by pasting his bookplate inside the cover. Having a fine library doesn't prove that its owner has a mind enriched by books; it proves nothing more than that he, his father, or his wife, was rich enough to buy them.

There are three kinds of book owners. The first has all the standard sets and best-sellers—unread, untouched. (This deluded individual owns woodpulp and ink, not books.) The second has a great many books—a few of them read through, most of them dipped into, but all of them as clean and shiny as the day they were bought. (This person would probably like to make books his own, but is restrained by a false respect for their physical appearance.) The third has a few books or many—everyone of them dog-eared and dilapidated, shaken and loosened by continual use, marked and scribbled in from front to back. (This man owns books.)

Is it false respect, you may ask, to preserve intact and unblemished a beautifully printed book, an elegantly bound edition? Of course not. I'd no more scribble all over a first edition of *Paradise Lost* than I'd give my baby a set of crayons and an original Rembrandt! I wouldn't mark up a painting or a statue. Its soul, so to speak, is inseparable from its body. And the beauty of a rare edition or of a richly manufactured volume is like that of a painting or a statue.

But the soul of a book *can* be separated from its body. A book is more like the score of a piece of music than it is like a painting. No great musician confuses a symphony with the printed sheets of music. Arturo Toscanini reveres Brahms, but Toscanini's score of the C-minor Symphony is so thoroughly marked up that no one but the maestro himself can read it. The reason why a great conductor makes notations on his musical scores—marks them up again and again each time he returns to study them—is the reason why you should mark your books.

If your respect for magnificent binding or typography gets in the way, buy yourself a cheap edition and pay your respects to the author.

Why is marking up a book indispensable to reading? First, it keeps you awake. (And I don't mean merely conscious; I mean wide awake.) In the second place, reading, if it is active, is thinking, and thinking tends to express itself in words, spoken or written. The marked book is usually the thought-through book. Finally, writing helps you remember the thoughts you had, or the thoughts the author expressed. Let me develop these three points.

If reading is to accomplish anything more than passing time, it must be active. You can't let your eyes glide across the lines of a book and come up with an understanding of what you have read. Now an ordinary piece of light fiction, like say, *Gone With the Wind,* doesn't require the most active kind of reading. The books you read for pleasure can be read in a state of relaxation, and nothing is lost. But a great book, rich in ideas and beauty, a book that raises and tries to answer great fundamental questions, demands the most active reading of which you are capable. You don't absorb the ideas of John Dewey the way you absorb the crooning of Mr. Vallee. You have to reach for them. That you cannot do while you're asleep.

If, when you've finished reading a book, the pages are filled with your notes, you know that you read actively. The most famous *active* reader of great books I know is President Hutchins, of the University of Chicago. He also has the hardest schedule of business activities of any man I know. He invariably reads with a pencil, and sometimes, when he picks up a book and pencil in the evening, he finds himself, instead of making intelligent notes, drawing what he calls "caviar factories" on the margins. When that happens, he puts the book down. He knows he's too tired to read, and he's just wasting time.

But, you may ask, why is writing necessary? Well, the physical act of writing, with your own hand, brings words and sentences more sharply before your mind and preserves them better in your memory. To set down your reaction to important words and sentences you have read, and the questions they have raised in your mind, is to preserve those reactions and sharpen those questions.

Even if you wrote on a scratch pad, and threw the paper away when you had finished writing, your grasp of the book would be surer. But you don't have to throw the paper away. The margins (top and bottom, as well as side), the end-papers, the very space between the lines, are all available. They aren't sacred. And, best of all, your marks and notes become an integral part of the book and stay there forever. You can pick up the book the following week or year, and there are all your points of agreement, disagreement, doubt, and inquiry. It's like resuming an interrupted conversation with the advantage of being able to pick up where you left off.

And that is exactly what reading a book should be: a conversation between you and the author. Presumably he knows more about the subject than you do; naturally, you'll have the proper humility as you approach him. But don't let anybody tell you that a reader is supposed to be solely on the receiving end. Understanding is a two-way operation; learning doesn't consist in being an empty receptacle. The learner has to question himself and question the teacher. He even has to argue with the teacher, once he understands what the teacher is saying. And marking a book is literally an expression of your differences, or agreements of opinion, with the author.

There are all kinds of devices for marking a book intelligently and fruitfully. Here's the way I do it:

1. *Underlining:* Of major points, of important or forceful statements.
2. *Vertical lines at the margin:* To emphasize a statement already underlined.
3. *Star, asterisk, or other doo-dad at the margin:* To be used sparingly, to emphasize the ten or twenty most important statements in the book. (You may want to fold the bottom corner of each page on which you use such marks. It won't hurt the sturdy paper on which most modern books are printed, and you will be able to take the book off the shelf at any time and, by opening it at the folded corner page, refresh your recollection of the book.)
4. *Numbers in the margin:* To indicate the sequence of points the author makes in developing a single argument.
5. *Numbers of other pages in the margin:* To indicate where else in the book the author made points relevant to the point marked; to tie up the ideas in a book, which, though they may be separated by many pages, belong together.
6. *Circling of key words or phrases.*
7. *Writing in the margin, or at the top or bottom of the page, for the sake of:* Recording questions (and perhaps answers) which a passage raised in your mind; reducing a complicated discussion to a simple statement; recording the sequence of major points right through the books. I use the end-papers at the back of the book

to make a personal index of the author's points in the order of their appearance.

The front end-papers are, to me, the most important. Some people reserve them for a fancy bookplate. I reserve them for fancy thinking. After I have finished reading the book and making my personal index on the back end-papers, I turn to the front and try to outline the book, not page by page, or point by point (I've already done that at the back), but as an integrated structure, with a basic unity and an order of parts. This outline is, to me, the measure of my understanding of the work.

If you're a die-hard anti-book-marker, you may object that the margins, the space between the lines, and the end-papers don't give you room enough. All right. How about using a scratch pad slightly smaller than the page-size of the book—so that the edges of the sheets won't protrude? Make your index, outlines, and even your notes on the pad, and then insert these sheets permanently inside the front and back covers of the book.

Or, you may say that this business of marking books is going to slow up your reading. It probably will. That's one of the reasons for doing it. Most of us have been taken in by the notion that speed of reading is a measure of our intelligence. There is no such thing as the right speed for intelligent reading. Some things should be read quickly and effortlessly, and some should be read slowly and even laboriously. The sign of intelligence in reading is the ability to read different things differently according to their worth. In the case of good books, the point is not to see how many of them you can get through, but rather how many can get through you—how many you can make your own. A few friends are better than a thousand acquaintances. If this be your aim, as it should be, you will not be impatient if it takes more time and effort to read a great book than it does a newspaper.

You may have one final objection to marking books. You can't lend them to your friends because nobody else can read them without being distracted by your notes. Furthermore, you won't want to lend them because a marked copy is a kind of intellectual diary, and lending it is almost like giving your mind away.

If your friend wishes to read your *Plutarch's Lives,* "Shakespeare," or *The Federalist Papers,* tell him gently but firmly to buy a copy. You will lend him your car or your coat—but your books are as much a part of you as your head or your heart.

Key Terms

mutilation
prelude
dilapidated
inseparable
maestro
indispensable
inquiry
interrupted
integrated

Questions on Meaning

1. This essay provides an argument for writing on the pages of books. The most important part of the argument is that it is the ideas in the books and not the paper that matter. How has the computer age made that more clear?
2. Why is it important to write in a book the ideas that you wish to remember? What should you write in the book, according to Adler? Do you write in your books?
3. Adler argues that a person ought not to lend a book to someone else. What would he think of reselling textbooks? Why do people resell their texts?

Questions on Rhetorical Strategy and Style

1. Adler clearly considers himself an expert on reading books. What evidence does he give that he is an expert reader?
2. In the middle of the essay, Adler compares making marks in expensive books to writing on paintings. Then he thinks better of the comparison and changes his object of comparison to music manuscripts. Why does he make this change?
3. Adler ends the essay with the following concept: writing in books enables the reader to have a conversation with the writer. What would have happened to your understanding of the essay if he had given this reason at the beginning?

Writing Assignments

1. Describe a book that you enjoyed reading. What made this book enjoyable for you? Have you read it more than once? Why?
2. Do you take notes in class? What kinds of notes do you take? For a week, take careful notes in one of your classes; then turn the notes into an essay about the content of the class for that week.
3. Why do some people consider some books special possessions? Ask your friends how their religions feel about their sacred books. Write about how these books are treated within the religion.

Everything Has a Name

Helen Keller

Helen Keller (1880–1968) was born in Tuscumbia, Alabama. As a result of illness, she lost her senses of sight and hearing at 19 months. Taught to speak, read, and write by Anne Sullivan, her teacher and lifelong companion, Keller graduated from Radcliffe (1904) at age 24. A symbol of personal strength and perseverance, Keller became a distinguished lecturer and writer. Her autobiography, The Story of My Life *(1902), was made into the award-winning film,* The Miracle Worker *(1959). This essay, excerpted from her autobiography, describes the moment when Keller understood the concept of language and reveals how that changed her life.*

1 The most important day I remember in all my life is the one on 1
which my teacher, Anne Mansfield Sullivan, came to me. I am filled with wonder when I consider the immeasurable contrast between the two lives which it connects. It was the third of March, 1887, three months before I was seven years old.

On the afternoon of that eventful day, I stood on the porch, dumb, expectant. I guessed vaguely from my mother's signs and from the hurrying to and fro in the house that something unusual was about to happen, so I went to the door and waited on the steps. The afternoon sun penetrated the mass of honeysuckle that covered the porch, and fell on my upturned face. My fingers lingered almost unconsciously on the familiar leaves and blossoms which had just come forth to greet the sweet southern spring. I did not know what the future held of marvel or surprise for me. Anger and bitterness had preyed upon me continually for weeks and a deep languor had succeeded this passionate struggle.

From *The Story of My Life* published by Doubleday, a division of Bantam Double Dell Publishing Groups, Inc.

Have you ever been at sea in a dense fog, when it seemed as if a tangible white darkness shut you in, and the great ship, tense and anxious, groped her way toward the shore with plummet and sounding-line, and you waited with beating heart for something to happen? I was like that ship before my education began, only I was without compass or sounding-line, and had no way of knowing how near the harbour was. "Light! give me light!" was the wordless cry of my soul, and the light of love shone on me in that very hour.

I felt approaching footsteps. I stretched out my hand as I supposed to my mother. Some one took it, and I was caught up and held close in the arms of her who had come to reveal all things to me, and, more than all things else, to love me.

5 The morning after my teacher came she led me into her room and gave me a doll. The little blind children at the Perkins Institution had sent it and Laura Bridgman [the first deaf and blind person to be educated in the United States] had dressed it; but I did not know this until afterward. When I had played with it a little while, Miss Sullivan slowly spelled into my hand the word "d-o-l-l." I was at once interested in this finger play and tried to imitate it. When I finally succeeded in making the letters correctly I was flushed with childish pleasure and pride. Running downstairs to my mother I held up my hand and made the letters for doll. I did not know that I was spelling a word or even that words existed: I was simply making my fingers go in monkey-like imitation. In the days that followed I learned to spell in this uncomprehending way a great many words, among them *pin, hat, cup,* and a few verbs like *sit, stand* and *walk.* But my teacher had been with me several weeks before I understood that everything has a name.

One day, while I was playing with my new doll, Miss Sullivan put my big rag doll into my lap also, spelled "d-o-l-l" and tried to make me understand that "d-o-l–l" applied to both. Earlier in the day we had had a tussle over the words "m-u-g" and "w-a-t-e-r." Miss Sullivan had tried to impress it upon me that "m-u-g" is *mug* and that "w-a-t-e-r" is *water,* but I persisted in confounding the two. In despair she had dropped the subject for the time, only to renew it at the first opportunity. I became impatient at her repeated attempts and, seizing the new doll, I dashed it upon the floor. I was keenly delighted when I felt the fragments of the broken doll at my feet. Neither sorrow nor regret followed my passionate outburst. I had not loved the doll. In the still, dark world in which I lived there was no strong sentiment or tenderness. I felt my teacher sweep the fragments to one side of the hearth, and I had a sense of satisfaction that the cause of my discomfort was removed. She brought me my hat, and I knew I was going out into the warm sunshine. This thought, if a wordless sensation may be called a thought, made me hop and skip with pleasure.

We walked down the path to the well-house, attracted by the fragrance of the honeysuckle with which it was covered. Some one was drawing water and my teacher placed my hand under the spout. As the cool stream gushed over one hand she spelled into the other the word *water,* first slowly, then rapidly. I stood still, my whole attention fixed upon the motions of her fingers. Suddenly I felt a misty consciousness as of something forgotten—a thrill of returning thought; and somehow the mystery of language was revealed to me. I knew then that "w-a-t-e-r" meant the wonderful cool something that was flowing over my hand. That living word awakened my soul, gave it light, hope, joy, set it free! There were barriers still, it is true, but barriers that could in time be swept away.

I left the well-house eager to learn. Everything had a name, and each name gave birth to a new thought. As we returned to the house every object which I touched seemed to quiver with life. That was because I saw everything with the strange, new sight that had come to me. On entering the door I remembered the doll I had broken. I felt my way to the hearth and picked up the pieces. I tried vainly to put them together. Then my eyes filled with tears; for I realized what I had done, and for the first time I felt repentance and sorrow.

I learned a great many new words that day. I do not remember what they all were; but I do know that *mother, father, sister, teacher* were among them—words that were to make the world blossom for me, "like Aaron's rod, with flowers." It would have been difficult to find a happier child than I was as I lay in my crib at the close of that eventful day and lived over the joys it had brought me, and for the first time longed for a new day to come.

Key Terms

expectant
immeasureable
lingered
plummet
languor
compass
spout
sounding-line
honeysuckle
Aaron's rod

Questions on Meaning

1. Perhaps more than anything, this selection is about language and its role in our lives. What is the significance of Keller's discovery that "everything has a name"?
2. Why do you imagine Keller had been angry and bitter in the time before Anne Sullivan arrived?
3. Why was Keller not bothered when she smashed her doll? Why did she later regret doing it?

Questions on Rhetorical Strategy and Style

1. Even though Keller had lost her sense of sight and hearing, her other senses remained alert. Look closely at the first four paragraphs and note the details that capture Keller's means of interacting with her environment. How could a blind person be so descriptive in her writing?
2. What is the tone of Keller's essay? What does it say about her as a person?
3. Keller is very careful to prepare the reader for her first encounter with Sullivan. Why? How did this encounter affect you?

Writing Assignments

1. Many of us have a story about a significant person in our lives. Write an essay or a profile, about such a person. Describe this person so readers can appreciate his or her physical appearance and character. What is your relationship with this person and how did he or she come into your life? What difference did this person make in your life?
2. The Keller story gives us a window into how people with disabilities were treated around the turn of the last century. Try writing a research paper in which you investigate this early treatment. Include in your research the role of the Perkins Institution. Were there others like it? How have the teaching of the deaf and blind changed today? How have the names we use to describe these conditions changed?

Learning to Read and Write

Frederick Douglass

Frederick Douglass (1817–1895)—abolitionist, author, and the first black American to become a prominent public figure—was born into slavery near Tuckahoe, Maryland. As a youth, Douglass worked as a household servant, a field hand, and a shipyard apprentice. In 1838, after several failed attempts to escape (for which he received beatings), he successfully reached New York. He took the surname "Douglass" and eventually settled in New Bedford, Massachusetts. In 1841, the Massachusetts Anti-Slavery League, impressed by his great oratory skills, hired Douglass to help promote the abolition of slavery. Douglass bought his freedom in 1847, using money contributed both by Americans and by sympathizers in England, where he had fled to preserve his freedom. For the next 13 years, Douglass edited the abolitionist periodical North Star *(changed to* Frederick Douglass's Paper *in 1851). During the Civil War, Douglass urged President Lincoln to emancipate the slaves and helped recruit black troops. After the war, he held a series of government posts, including Assistant Secretary to the Santo Domingo Commission, Marshall of the District of Columbia, District Recorder of Deeds, and Ambassador to Haiti. This essay, which comes from Douglass's autobiography,* Narrative of the Life of Frederick Douglass, an American Slave *(1845), reveals the guile and determination that Douglass employed to teach himself to read. As you read the words of a former slave, written more than a century ago, think of how closed the world was to Douglass, yet how he recognized that literacy could help open the door.*

1 I lived in Master Hugh's family about seven years. During this time, 1
I succeeded in learning to read and write. In accomplishing this, I was compelled to resort to various stratagems. I had no regular teacher. My mistress, who had kindly commenced to instruct me, had, in compliance with the advice and direction of her husband, not only ceased to instruct, but had set her face against my being instructed by any one else. It is due, however, to my mistress to say of her, that she did not adopt this course of treatment immediately. She at first lacked the depravity indispensable to shutting me up in mental darkness. It was at least necessary for her to have some training in the exercise of irresponsible power, to make her equal to the task of treating me as though I were a brute.

My mistress was, as I have said, a kind and tender-hearted woman; and in the simplicity of her soul she commenced, when I first went to live with her, to treat me as she supposed one human being ought to treat another. In entering upon the duties of a slaveholder, she did not seem to perceive that I sustained to her the relation of a mere chattel, and that for her to treat me as a human being was not only wrong, but dangerously so. Slavery proved as injurious to her as it did to me. When I went there, she was a pious, warm, and tender-hearted woman. There was no sorrow or suffering for which she had not a tear. She had bread for the hungry, clothes for the naked, and comfort for every mourner that came within her reach. Slavery soon proved its ability to divest her of these heavenly qualities. Under its influence, the tender heart became stone, and the lamb-like disposition gave way to one of tiger-like fierceness. The first step in her downward course was in her ceasing to instruct me. She now commenced to practise her husband's precepts. She finally became even more violent in her opposition than her husband himself. She was not satisfied with simply doing as well as he had commanded; she seemed anxious to do better. Nothing seemed to make her more angry than to see me with a newspaper. She seemed to think that here lay the danger. I have had her rush at me with a face made all up of fury, and snatch from me a newspaper, in a manner that fully revealed her apprehension. She was an apt woman; and a little experience soon demonstrated, to her satisfaction, that education and slavery were incompatible with each other.

From this time I was most narrowly watched. If I was in a separate room any considerable length of time, I was sure to be suspected of having a book, and was at once called to give an account of myself. All this, however, was too late. The first step had been taken. Mistress, in teaching me the alphabet, had given me the *inch,* and no precaution could prevent me from taking the *ell.*

The plan which I adopted, and the one by which I was most successful, was that of making friends of all the little white boys whom I met in the street. As many of these as I could, I converted into teachers. With their kindly aid, obtained at different times and in different places, I finally succeeded in learning to read. When I was sent on errands, I always took my book with me, and by going one part of my errand quickly, I found time to get a lesson before my return. I used also to carry bread with me, enough of which was always in the house, and to which I was always welcome; for I was much better off in this regard than many of the poor white children in our neighborhood. This bread I used to bestow upon the hungry little urchins, who, in return, would give me that more valuable bread of knowledge. I am strongly tempted to give the names of two or three of those little boys, as a testimonial of the gratitude and affection I bear them; but prudence forbids;—not that it would injure me, but it might embarrass them; for it is almost an unpardonable offense to teach slaves to read in this Christian country. It is enough to say of the dear little fellows, that they lived on Philpot Street, very near Durgin and Bailey's shipyard. I used to talk this matter of slavery over with them. I would sometimes say to them, I wished I could be as free as they would be when they got to be men. "You will be free as soon as you are twenty-one, *but I am a slave for life!* Have not I as good a right to be free as you have?" These words used to trouble them; they would express for me the liveliest sympathy, and console me with the hope that something would occur by which I might be free.

5 I was now about twelve years old, and the thought of being *a slave* 5
for life began to bear heavily upon my heart. Just about this time, I got hold of a book entitled "The Columbian Orator." Every opportunity I got, I used to read this book. Among much of other interesting matter, I found in it a dialogue between a master and his slave. The slave was represented as having run away from his master three times. The dialogue represented the conversation which took place between them, when the slave was retaken the third time. In this dialogue, the whole argument in behalf of slavery was brought forward by the master, all of which was disposed of by the slave. The slave was made to

say some very smart as well as impressive things in reply to his master—things which had the desired though unexpected effect; for the conversation resulted in the voluntary emancipation of the slave on the part of the master.

In the same book, I met with one of Sheridan's mighty speeches on and in behalf of Catholic emancipation. These were choice documents to me. I read them over and over again with unabated interest. They gave tongue to interesting thoughts of my own soul, which had frequently flashed through my mind, and died away for want of utterance. The moral which I gained from the dialogue was the power of truth over the conscience of even a slaveholder. What I got from Sheridan was a bold denunciation of slavery, and a powerful vindication of human rights. The reading of these documents enabled me to utter my thoughts, and to meet the arguments brought forward to sustain slavery; but while they relieved me of one difficulty, they brought on another even more painful than the one of which I was relieved. The more I read, the more I was led to abhor and detest my enslavers. I could regard them in no other light than a band of successful robbers, who had left their homes, and gone to Africa, and stolen us from our homes, and in a strange land reduced us to slavery. I loathed them as being the meanest as well as the most wicked of men. As I read and contemplated the subject, behold! that very discontentment which Master Hugh had predicted would follow my learning to read had already come, to torment and sting my soul to unutterable anguish. As I writhed under it, I would at times feel that learning to read had been a curse rather than a blessing. It had given me a view of my wretched condition, without the remedy. It opened my eyes to the horrible pit, but to no ladder upon which to get out. In moments of agony, I envied my fellow-slaves for their stupidity. I have often wished myself a beast. I preferred the condition of the meanest reptile to my own. Any thing, no matter what, to get rid of thinking! It was this everlasting thinking of my condition that tormented me. There was no getting rid of it. It was pressed upon me by every object within sight or hearing, animate or inanimate. The silver trump of freedom had roused my soul to eternal wakefulness. Freedom now appeared, to disappear no more forever. It was heard in every sound, and seen in every thing. It was ever present to torment me with a sense of my wretched condition. I saw nothing without seeing it, I heard nothing without hearing it, and felt nothing without feeling it. It looked from every star, it smiled in every calm, breathed in every wind, and moved in every storm.

I often found myself regretting my own existence, and wishing myself dead; and but for the hope of being free, I have no doubt but that I should have killed myself, or done something for which I should have been killed. While in this state of mind, I was eager to hear any one speak of slavery. I was a ready listener. Every little while, I could hear something about the abolitionists. It was some time before I found what the word meant. It was always used in such connections as to make it an interesting word to me. If a slave ran away and succeeded in getting clear, or if a slave killed his master, set fire to a barn, or did any thing very wrong in the mind of a slaveholder, it was spoken of as the fruit of *abolition.* Hearing the word in this connection very often, I set about learning what it meant. The dictionary afforded me little or no help. I found it was "the act of abolishing," but then I did not know what was to be abolished. Here I was perplexed. I did not dare to ask any one about its meaning, for I was satisfied that it was something they wanted me to know very little about. After a patient waiting, I got one of our city papers, containing an account of the number of petitions from the north, praying for the abolition of slavery in the District of Columbia, and of the slave trade between the States. From this time I understood the words *abolition* and *abolitionist,* and always drew near when that word was spoken, expecting to hear something of importance to myself and fellow-slaves. The light broke in upon me by degrees. I went one day down on the wharf of Mr. Waters; and seeing two Irishmen unloading a scow of stone, I went, unasked, and helped them. When we had finished, one of them came to me and asked me if I were a slave. I told him I was. He asked, "Are ye a slave for life?" I told him that I was. The good Irishman seemed to be deeply affected by the statement. He said to the other that it was a pity so fine a little fellow as myself should be a slave for life. He said it was a shame to hold me. They both advised me to run away to the north; that I should find friends there, and that I should be free. I pretended not to be interested in what they said, and treated them as if I did not understand them; for I feared they might be treacherous. White men have been known to encourage slaves to escape, and then, to get the reward, catch them and return them to their masters. I was afraid that these seemingly good men might use me so; but I nevertheless remembered their advice, and from that time I resolved to run away. I looked forward to a time at which it would be safe for me to escape. I was too young to think of doing so immediately; besides, I wished to learn how to write, as I might have occasion to write my own pass. I consoled myself with the hope that I should one day find a good chance. Meanwhile, I would learn to write.

The idea as to how I might learn to write was suggested to me by being in Durgin and Bailey's ship-yard, and frequently seeing the ship carpenters, after hewing, and getting a piece of timber ready for use, write on the timber the name of that part of the ship for which it was intended. When a piece of timber was intended for the larboard side, it would be marked thus—"L." When a piece was for the starboard side, it would be marked thus—"S." A piece for the larboard side forward, would be marked thus—"L. F." When a piece was for starboard side forward, it would be marked thus—"S. F." For larboard aft, it would be marked thus—"L. A." For starboard aft, it would be marked thus—"S. A." I soon learned the names of these letters, and for what they were intended when placed upon a piece of timber in the shipyard. I immediately commenced copying them, and in a short time was able to make the four letters named. After that, when I met with any boy who I knew could write, I would tell him I could write as well as he. The next word would be, "I don't believe you. Let me see you try it." I would then make the letters which I had been so fortunate as to learn, and ask him to beat that. In this way I got a good many lessons in writing, which it is quite possible I should never have gotten in any other way. During this time, my copy-book was the board fence, brick wall, and pavement; my pen and ink was a lump of chalk. With these, I learned mainly how to write. I then commenced and continued copying the Italics in Webster's Spelling Book, until I could make them all without looking on the book. By this time, my little Master Thomas had gone to school, and learned how to write, and had written over a number of copy-books. These had been brought home, and shown to some of our near neighbors, and then laid aside. My mistress used to go to class meeting at the Wilk Street meetinghouse every Monday afternoon, and leave me to take care of the house. When left thus, I used to spend the time in writing in the spaces left in Master Thomas's copy-book, copying what he had written. I continued to do this until I could write a hand very similar to that of Master Thomas. Thus, after a long, tedious effort for years, I finally succeeded in learning how to write.

Key Terms

stratagems
depravity
chattel
precepts
ell
bestow
prudence
emancipation
unabated
abolitionists

Questions on Meaning

1. Douglass tells of the moral fall of his mistress who knows the wife of the man who owned Douglass. What happened to her because she owned slaves?
2. For Douglass, learning to read and write both came through trickery. How did he trick the children he knew into helping him learn to read? How did he learn to write from watching others and using their work?
3. Douglass read about abolition, the idea of freeing the slaves. What happened to him after he realized that he could be free by running away? Why was he actually less happy for having learned about possible freedom?

Questions on Rhetorical Strategy and Style

1. This essay is written in the first person. How does Douglass change his tone as he moves through the essay? Note that he talks about himself as a youngster at the beginning and goes on through his young adulthood.
2. Sometimes Douglass uses sarcasm to get his point across. He talks about how his mistress learned to be a slave owner as if she actually were getting to be good at something. In what other places does Douglass show this kind of sarcastic tone, and why does he do this?

3. The essays divides neatly into the experience of learning to read and then the experience of learning to write. How does this organization help the reader to understand the difficulties of both processes?

Writing Assignments

1. Today many African Americans are talking about the idea of reparations, or repaying slaves' grandchildren and great grandchildren for the wrongs suffered. Write an essay that looks carefully at the pros and cons of this idea.
2. We, like Douglass's mistress, all have to be carefully taught to behave badly. What messages does our culture give us about bad behavior that is approved? (Hint: how are we taught by the culture to feel about being poor or overweight or not-so-very-beautiful?)

Me Talk Pretty One Day

David Sedaris

David Sedaris is considered a master of satire and his readings sell out concert halls across the country. He has a CD entitled David Sedaris at Carnegie Hall. *He read his stories on stage and on the radio, and has had plays produced in New York at La Mama and at Lincoln Center. He has written essays for* Esquire *and* The New Yorker. *His works include* Book of Liz *(2002),* Me Talk Pretty One Day *(2001),* Holidays on Ice *(1998) and* Naked *(1998). He won an Obie Award for a theater production created with his sister, Amy Sedaris, called* One Women Shoe. *Sedaris is a regular contributor to National Public Radio's "This American Life."*

1 At the age of forty-one, I am returning to school and have to 1
think of myself as what my French textbook calls "a true debutant." After paying my tuition, I was issued a student ID, which allows me a discounted entry fee at movie theaters, puppet shows, and Festyland, a far-flung amusement park that advertises with billboards picturing a cartoon stegosaurus sitting in a canoe and eating what appears to be a ham sandwich.

I've moved to Paris with hope of learning the language. My school is an easy ten-minute walk from my apartment, and on the first day of class I arrived early, watching as the returning students greeted one another in the school lobby. Vacations were recounted, and questions were raised concerning mutual friends with names like Kang and Vlatnya. Regardless of their nationalities, everyone spoke in

---

what sounded to me like excellent French. Some accents were better than others, but the students exhibited an ease and confidence I found intimidating. As an added discomfort, they were all young, attractive, and well dressed, causing me to feel not unlike Pa Kettle trapped backstage after a fashion show.

The first day of class was nerve-racking because I knew I'd be expected to perform. That's the way they do it here—it's everybody into the language pool, sink or swim. The teacher marched in, deeply tanned from a recent vacation, and proceeded to rattle off a series of administrative announcements. I've spent quite a few summers in Normandy, and I took a monthlong French class before leaving New York. I'm not completely in the dark, yet I understood only half of what this woman was saying.

"If you have not *meimslsxp* or *lgpdmurct* by this time, then you should not be in this room. Has everyone *apzkiubjxow?* Everyone? Good, we shall begin." She spread out her lesson plan and sighed, saying, "All right, then, who knows the alphabet?"

It was startling because (a) I hadn't been asked that question in a while and (b) I realized, while laughing, that I myself did *not* know the alphabet. They're the same letters, but in France they're pronounced differently. I know the shape of the alphabet but had no idea what it actually sounded like.

"Ahh." The teacher went to the board and sketched the letter *a.* "Do we have anyone in the room whose first name commences with an *ahh?*"

Two Polish Annas raised their hands, and the teacher instructed them to present themselves by stating their names, nationalities, occupations, and a brief list of things they liked and disliked in this world. The first Anna hailed from an industrial town outside of Warsaw and had front teeth the size of tombstones. She worked as a seamstress, enjoyed quiet times with friends, and hated the mosquito.

"Oh, really," the teacher said. "How very interesting. I thought that everyone loved the mosquito, but here, in front of all the world, you claim to detest him. How is it that we've been blessed with someone as unique and original as you? Tell us, please."

The seamstress did not understand what was being said but knew that this was an occasion for shame. Her rabbity mouth huffed for breath, and she stared down at her lap as though the appropriate comeback were stitched somewhere alongside the zipper of her slacks.

10 The second Anna learned from the first and claimed to love sunshine and detest lies. It sounded like a translation of one of those Playmate of the Month data sheets, the answers always written in the same loopy handwriting: "Turn-ons: Mom's famous five-alarm chili! Turnoffs: insecurity and guys who come on too strong!!!!"

The two Polish Annas surely had clear notions of what they loved and hated, but like the rest of us, they were limited in terms of vocabulary, and this made them appear less than sophisticated. The teacher forged on, and we learned that Carlos, the Argentine bandonion player, loved wine, music, and in his words, "making sex with the womens of the world." Next came a beautiful young Yugoslav who identified herself as an optimist, saying that she loved everything that life had to offer.

The teacher licked her lips, revealing a hint of the saucebox we would later come to know. She crouched low for her attack, placed her hands on the young woman's desk, and leaned close, saying, "Oh yeah? And do you love your little war?"

While the optimist struggled to defend herself, I scrambled to think of an answer to what had obviously become a trick question. How often is one asked what he loves in this world? More to the point, how often is one asked and then publicly ridiculed for his answer? I recalled my mother, flushed with wine, pounding the tabletop late one night, saying, "Love? I love a good steak cooked rare. I love my cat, and I love . . ." My sisters and I leaned forward, waiting to hear our names. "Tums," our mother said. "I love Tums."

The teacher killed some time accusing the Yugoslavian girl of masterminding a program of genocide, and I jotted frantic notes in the margins of my pad. While I can honestly say that I love leafing through medical textbooks devoted to severe dermatological conditions, the hobby is beyond the reach of my French vocabulary, and acting it out would only have invited controversy.

15 When called upon, I delivered an effortless list of things that I detest: blood sausage, intestinal pâtés, brain pudding. I'd learned these words the hard way. Having given it some thought, I then declared my love for IBM typewriters, the French word for *bruise,* and my electric floor waxer. It was a short list, but still I managed to mispronounce *IBM* and assign the wrong gender to both the floor waxer and the typewriter. The teacher's reaction led me to believe that these mistakes were capital crimes in the country of France.

"Were you always this *palicmkrexis?*" she asked. "Even a *fiuscrzsa ticiwelmun* knows that a typewriter is feminine."

I absorbed as much of her abuse as I could understand, thinking—but not saying—that I find it ridiculous to assign a gender to an inanimate object incapable of disrobing and making an occasional fool of itself. Why refer to Lady Crack Pipe or Good Sir Dishrag when these things could never live up to all that their sex implied?

The teacher proceeded to belittle everyone from German Eva, who hated laziness, to Japanese Yukari, who loved paintbrushes and soap. Italian, Thai, Dutch, Korean, and Chinese—we all left class foolishly believing that the worst was over. She'd shaken us up a little, but surely that was just an act designed to weed out the deadweight. We didn't know it then, but the coming months would teach us what it was like to spend time in the presence of a wild animal, something completely unpredictable. Her temperament was not based on a series of good and bad days but, rather, good and bad moments. We soon learned to dodge chalk and protect our heads and stomachs whenever she approached us with a question. She hadn't yet punched anyone, but it seemed wise to protect ourselves against the inevitable.

Though we were forbidden to speak anything but French, the teacher would occasionally use us to practice any of her five fluent languages.

"I hate you," she said to me one afternoon. Her English was flawless. "I really, really hate you." Call me sensitive, but I couldn't help but take it personally.

After being singled out as a lazy *kfdtinvfm,* I took to spending four hours a night on my homework, putting in even more time whenever we were assigned an essay. I suppose I could have gotten by with less, but I was determined to create some sort of identity for myself: David the hard worker, David the cut-up. We'd have one of those "complete this sentence" exercises, and I'd fool with the thing for hours, invariably settling on something like "A quick run around the lake? I'd love to! Just give me a moment while I strap on my wooden leg." The teacher, through word and action, conveyed the message that if this was my idea of an identity, she wanted nothing to do with it.

My fear and discomfort crept beyond the borders of the classroom and accompanied me out onto the wide boulevards. Stopping for a coffee, asking directions, depositing money in my bank account:

these things were out of the question, as they involved having to speak. Before beginning school, there'd been no shutting me up, but now I was convinced that everything I said was wrong. When the phone rang, I ignored it. If someone asked me a question, I pretended to be deaf. I knew my fear was getting the best of me when I started wondering why they don't sell cuts of meat in vending machines.

My only comfort was the knowledge that I was not alone. Huddled in the hallways and making the most of our pathetic French, my fellow students and I engaged in the sort of conversation commonly overheard in refugee camps.

"Sometime me cry alone at night."

"That be common for I, also, but be more strong, you. Much work and someday you talk pretty. People start love you soon. Maybe tomorrow, okay."

Unlike the French class I had taken in New York, here there was no sense of competition. When the teacher poked a shy Korean in the eyelid with a freshly sharpened pencil, we took no comfort in the fact that, unlike Hyeyoon Cho, we all knew the irregular past tense of the verb *to defeat.* In all fairness, the teacher hadn't meant to stab the girl, but neither did she spend much time apologizing, saying only, "Well, you should have been *vkkdyo* more *kdeynfulh.*"

Over time it became impossible to believe that any of us would ever improve. Fall arrived and it rained every day, meaning we would now be scolded for the water dripping from our coats and umbrellas. It was mid-October when the teaching singled me out, saying, "Every day spent with you is like having a cesarean section." And it struck me that, for the first time since arriving in France, I could understand every word that someone was saying.

Understanding doesn't mean that you can suddenly speak the language. Far from it. It's a small step, nothing more, yet its rewards are intoxicating and deceptive. The teacher continued her diatribe and I settled back, bathing in the subtle beauty of each new curse and insult.

"You exhaust me with your foolishness and reward my efforts with nothing but pain, do you understand me?"

The world opened up, and it was with great joy that I responded, "I know the thing that you speak exact now. Talk me more, you, plus, please, plus."

Questions on Meaning

1. Have you ever been in a situation where you could not fluently speak a language and thus felt awkward and powerless? What was this experience like for you? Explain in detail. How did you manage to maintain your sense of identity?
2. Explain the attitude of the teacher. It appears plainly rude, but it is also a reflection of more complicated and problematic traditions. As students, what do you make of the teacher's behavior?
3. What understanding does the author come to at the end? What "world opened up" and why was it joyful?

Questions on Rhetorical Strategy and Style

1. An important characteristic of this essay is its humor. What manner of humor is it? How does it serve to advance the author's perspective?
2. When the teacher asks the students if they know the alphabet, the author realizes that he does not. What is the symbolic significance of this reference to the basic units of language?
3. A good portion of the essay is devoted to the two Annas, the Argentine bandonion player, and the Yugoslav optimist. What purpose do they serve the essay? Discuss each one separately.

Writing Assignments

1. The author's experience might be unusual in some respects, but in one sense, it is a typical story of the return of a so-called non-traditional student. If you have a similar experience, write an essay describing it. If you know such a student, interview him or her and write a profile of that person's experiences.
2. The essay is an example of a literacy narrative. These are essays that describe someone's experience with acquiring a literacy that results in empowerment. A famous example of such a narrative is the essay "Learning to Read and Write" by Frederick Douglass. Write your own narrative of how you came to be a reader and a writer. In your essay, detail specific experiences that illustrate your story.

Mother Tongue

Amy Tan

Amy Tan was born in Oakland, California in 1952, several years after her mother and father immigrated from China. She was raised in various cities in the San Francisco Bay Area. When she was eight, her essay, "What the Library Means to Me," won first prize among elementary school participants, for which Tan received a transistor radio and publication in the local newspaper. Upon the deaths of her brother and father in 1967 and 1968 from brain tumors, the family began a haphazard journey through Europe, before settling in Montreux, Switzerland, where Tan graduated in her junior year in 1969.

For the next seven years, Tan attended five schools. She first went to Linfield College in McMinnville, Oregon, and there, on a blind date, met her future husband, Lou DeMattei. She followed him to San Jose, where she enrolled in San Jose City College. She next attended San Jose State University, and, while working two part-time jobs, she became an English honor's students and a President's Scholar, while carrying a semester course load of 21 units. In 1972 she graduated with honors, receiving a B.A. with a double major in English and Linguistics. She was awarded a scholarship to attend the Summer Linguistics Institute at the University of California, Santa Cruz. In 1973, she earned her M.A. in Linguistics, also from San Jose State University, and was then awarded a Graduate Minority Fellowship under the affirmative action program at the University of California, Berkeley, where she enrolled as a doctoral student in linguistics.

---

1 I am not a scholar of English or literature. I cannot give you much more than personal opinions on the English language and its variations in this country or others. 1

I am a writer. And by that definition, I am someone who has always loved language. I am fascinated by language in daily life. I spend a great deal of my time thinking about the power of language—the way it can evoke an emotion, a visual image, a complex idea, or a simple truth. Language is the tool of my trade. And I use them all—all the Englishes I grew up with.

Recently, I was made keenly aware of the different Englishes I do use. I was giving a talk to a large group of people, the same talk I had already given to half a dozen other groups. The nature of the talk was about my writing, my life, and my book, *The Joy Luck Club.* The talk was going along well enough, until I remembered one major difference that made the whole talk sound wrong. My mother was in the room. And it was perhaps the first time she had heard me give a lengthy speech, using the kind of English I have never used with her. I was saying things like, "The intersection of memory upon imagination" and "There is an aspect of my fiction that relates to thus-and-thus"—a speech filled with carefully wrought grammatical phrases, burdened, it suddenly seemed to me, with nominalized forms, past perfect tenses, conditional phrases, all the forms of standard English that I had learned in school and through books, the forms of English I did not use at home with my mother.

Just last week, I was walking down the street with my mother, and I again found myself conscious of the English I was using, and the English I do use with her. We were talking about the price of new and used furniture and I heard myself saying this: "Not waste money that way." My husband was with us as well, and he didn't notice any switch in my English. And then I realized why. It's because over the twenty years we've been together I've often used that same kind of English with him, and sometimes he even uses it with me. It has become our language of intimacy, a different sort of English that relates to family talk, the language I grew up with.

5 So you'll have some idea of what this family talk I heard sounds like, I'll quote what my mother said during a recent conversation which I videotaped and then transcribed. During this conversation, my mother was talking about a political gangster in Shanghai who had the same last name as her family's, Du, and how the gangster in his 5

early years wanted to be adopted by her family, which was rich by comparison. Later, the gangster became more powerful, far richer than my mother's family, and one day showed up at my mother's wedding to pay his respects. Here's what she said in part:

"Du Yusong having business like fruit stand. Like off the street kind. He is Du like Du Zong—but not Tsung-ming Island people. The local people call putong, the river east side, he belong to that side local people. That man want to ask Du Zong father take him in like become own family. Du Zong father wasn't look down on him, but didn't take seriously, until that man big like become a mafia. Now important person, very hard to inviting him. Chinese way, came only to show respect, don't stay for dinner. Respect for making big celebration, he shows up. Mean gives lots of respect. Chinese custom. Chinese social life that way. If too important won't have to stay too long. He come to my wedding. I didn't see, I heard it. I gone to boy's side, they have YMCA dinner. Chinese age I was nineteen."

You should know that my mother's expressive command of English belies how much she actually understands. She reads the *Forbes* report, listens to *Wall Street Week*, converses daily with her stockbroker, reads all of Shirley MacLaine's books with ease—all kinds of things I can't begin to understand. Yet some of my friends tell me they understand 50 percent of what my mother says. Some say they understand 80 to 90 percent. Some say they understand none of it, as if she were speaking pure Chinese. But to me, my mother's English is perfectly clear, perfectly natural. It's my mother tongue. Her language, as I hear it, is vivid, direct, full of observation and imagery. That was the language that helped shape the way I saw things, expressed things, made sense of the world.

Lately, I've been giving more thought to the kind of English my mother speaks. Like others, I have described it to people as "broken" or "fractured" English. But I wince when I say that. It has always bothered me that I can think of no way to describe it other than "broken," as if it were damaged and needed to be fixed, as if it lacked a certain wholeness and soundness. I've heard other terms used, "limited English," for example. But they seem just as bad, as if everything is limited, including people's perceptions of the limited English speaker.

I know this for a fact, because when I was growing up, my mother's "limited" English limited *my* perception of her. I was ashamed of her English. I believed that her English reflected the quality of what she had to say. That is, because she expressed them imperfectly her thoughts were imperfect. And I had plenty of empirical evidence to support me: the fact that people in department stores, at banks, and at restaurants did not take her seriously, did not give her good service, pretended not to understand her, or even acted as if they did not hear her.

My mother has long realized the limitations of her English as well. When I was fifteen, she used to have me call people on the phone to pretend I was she. In this guise, I was forced to ask for information or even to complain and yell at people who had been rude to her. One time it was a call to her stockbroker in New York. She had cashed out her small portfolio and it just so happened we were going to go to New York the next week, our very first trip outside California. I had to get on the phone and say in an adolescent voice that was not very convincing, "This is Mrs. Tan."

And my mother was standing in the back whispering loudly, "Why he don't send me check, already two weeks late. So mad he lie to me, losing me money."

And then I said in perfect English, "Yes, I'm getting rather concerned. You had agreed to send the check two weeks ago, but it hasn't arrived."

Then she began to talk more loudly. "What he want, I come to New York tell him front of his boss, you cheating me?" And I was trying to calm her down, make her be quiet, while telling the stockbroker, "I can't tolerate any more excuses. If I don't receive the check immediately, I am going to have to speak to your manager when I'm in New York next week." And sure enough, the following week there we were in front of this astonished stockbroker, and I was sitting there red-faced and quiet, and my mother, the real Mrs. Tan, was shouting at his boss in her impeccable broken English.

We used a similar routine just five days ago, for a situation that was far less humorous. My mother had gone to the hospital for an appointment, to find out about a benign brain tumor a CAT scan had revealed a month ago. She said she had spoken very good English, her best English, no mistakes. Still, she said, the hospital did not apologize when they said they had lost the CAT scan and she had come for nothing. She said they did not seem to have any sympathy when she told them she was anxious to know the exact diagnosis, since her husband and son had both died of brain tumors. She said they would not give her any more information until the next time and she would have to make another appointment for that. So she said she would not leave until the doctor called her daughter. She wouldn't budge. And when the doctor finally called her daughter, me, who spoke in perfect English—lo and behold—we had assurances the CAT scan would be found, promises that a conference call on Monday would be held, and apologies for any suffering my mother had gone through for a most regrettable mistake.

15 I think my mother's English almost had an effect on limiting my 15 possibilities in life as well. Sociologists and linguists probably will tell you that a person's developing language skills are more influenced by peers. But I do think that the language spoken in the family, especially in immigrant families which are more insular, plays a large role in shaping the language of the child. And I believe that it affected my results on achievement tests, IQ tests, and the SAT. While my English skills were never judged as poor, compared to math, English could not be considered my strong suit. In grade school I did moderately well, getting perhaps B's, sometimes B-pluses, in English and scoring perhaps in the sixtieth or seventieth percentile on achievement tests. But those scores were not good enough to override the opinion that my true abilities lay in math and science, because in those areas I achieved A's and scored in the ninetieth percentile or higher.

This was understandable. Math is precise, there is only one correct answer. Whereas, for me at least, the answers on English tests were always a judgment call, a matter of opinion and personal experience. Those tests were constructed around items like fill-in-the-blank sentence completion, Such as, "Even though Tom was __________, Mary thought he was __________." And the correct answer always seemed to be the most bland combinations of thoughts, for example, "Even though Tom was shy, Mary thought he was charming," with the grammatical structure "even though" limiting the correct answer to some sort of semantic opposites, so you wouldn't get answers like, Even though Tom was foolish, Mary thought he was ridiculous." Well, according to my mother, there were very few limitations as to what Tom could have been and what Mary might have thought of him. So I never did well on tests like that.

The same was true with word analogies, pairs of words in which you were supposed to find some sort of logical, semantic relationship—

for example, "*Sunset* is to *nightfall* as ________ is to ________." And here you would be presented with a list of four possible pairs, one of which showed the same kind of relationship: *red* is to *stoplight, bus* is to *arrival, chills* is to *fever, yawn* is to *boring.* Well, I could never think that way. I knew what the tests were asking, but I could not block out of my mind the images already created by the first pair, "*sunset* is to *nightfall*"—and I would see a burst of colors against a darkening sky, the moon rising, the lowering of a curtain of stars. And all the other pairs of words—red, bus, stoplight, boring—just threw up a mass of confusing images, making it impossible for me to sort out something as logical as saying: "A sunset precedes nightfall" is the same as "a chill precedes a fever." The only way I would have gotten that answer right would have been to imagine an associative situation, for example, my being disobedient and staying out past sunset, catching a chill at night, which turns into feverish pneumonia as punishment, which indeed did happen to me.

I have been thinking about all this lately, about my mother's English, about achievement tests. Because lately I've been asked, as a writer, why there are not more Asian Americans represented in American literature. Why are there few Asian Americans enrolled in creative writing programs? Why do so many Chinese students go into engineering? Well, these are broad sociological questions I can't begin to answer. But I have noticed in surveys—in fact, just last week—that Asian students, as a whole, always do significantly better on math achievement tests than in English. And this makes me think that there are other Asian American students whose English spoken in the home might also be described as "broken" or "limited." And perhaps they also have teachers who are steering them away from writing and into math and science, which is what happened to me.

Fortunately, I happen to be rebellious in nature and enjoy the challenge of disproving assumptions made about me. I became an English major my first year in college, after being enrolled as pre-med. I started writing nonfiction as a freelancer the week after I was told by my former boss that writing was my worst skill and I should hone my talents toward account management.

20 But it wasn't until 1985 that I finally began to write fiction. And at first I wrote using what I thought to be wittily crafted sentences, sentences that would finally prove I had mastery over the English

language. Here's an example from the first draft of a story that later made its way into *The Joy Luck Club,* but without this line: "That was my mental quandary in its nascent state." A terrible line, which I can barely pronounce.

Fortunately, for reasons I won't get into today, I later decided I should envision a reader for the stories I would write. And the reader I decided upon was my mother, because these were stories about mothers. So with this reader in mind—and in fact she did read my early drafts—I began to write stories using all the Englishes I grew up with: the English I spoke to my mother, which for lack of a better term might be described as "simple"; the English she used with me, which for lack of a better term might be described as "broken"; my translation of her Chinese, which could certainly be described as "watered down"; and what I imagined to be her translation of her Chinese if she could speak in perfect English, her internal language, and for that I sought to preserve the essence, but neither an English nor a Chinese structure. I wanted to capture what language ability tests can never reveal: her intent, her passion, her imagery, the rhythms of her speech and the nature of her thoughts.

Apart from what any critic had to say about my writing, I knew I had succeeded where it counted when my mother finished reading my book and gave me her verdict: "So easy to read."

Key Terms

evoke
intersection
nominalized
transcribed
putong
perceptions
empirical
guise
impeccable
nascent

Questions on Meaning

1. Amy Tan's mother is Chinese. This essay is about how Amy grew from being embarrassed by her mother to being an admirer of her mother. What shows that Tan came to admire her mother?
2. The mother in the essay uses a mixed dialect of Chinese word order and word choice combined with English words. Tan says that the dialect creates closeness in her family when they use it. Why does a family dialect help the create this closeness?
3. Tan contends that her mother understands more about the world of business and economics than Tan does. What proof does she use to show her mother's knowledge?

Questions on Rhetorical Strategy and Style

1. Tan uses several examples of her mother's dialect. How does this use of language help to bring the point of the essay home to the reader?
2. In the center of the essay, Tan seems to add another subject, her achievement on tests and her abilities in math and science. Why does she spend time in this essay on her achievement in these areas? What does this example prove?
3. The essay begins with a statement of lack of authority. Tan first says that she is not a scholar of English; she then goes on to show

that she is truly an English scholar. Why does she begin the essay this way? What does she hope to show to her reader?

Writing Assignments

1. Why are children, especially children in their teens and twenties, often embarrassed by their parents? Think of a situation when your parent embarrassed you and describe the situation. Then analyze why you reacted the way you did. What insecurities were you feeling and why you were experiencing them?
2. Research your family history and write about your family tree. Who were your ancestors? Where did they come from and why? Go as far back as you can (you may have to ask your parents and other relatives).
3. Who reads what you write? Write about your various audiences. Who would be interested in what you know and can do?

What Is Intelligence, Anyway?

Isaac Asimov

Isaac Asimov (1920–1992) was born in Russia but grew up in America. He received his Ph.D. in chemistry from Columbia University and thereafter taught biochemistry. He is better known as a science and science fiction writer. His three Foundation *novels were published in the 1950s, followed by the* Robot *novels and literally dozens of additional novels, collections of short stories, popular science books, and essays. Although educated as a scientific specialist and academician, Asimov always made it his goal to write for nonspecialized readers. He is perhaps best known for his writing—both nonfiction and fiction—that explains scientific concepts and realities for the general public. You will see that quality in this essay, which addresses the question of what intelligence really is. The essay is obviously written for a general reader and avoids technical or scientific discussion of intelligence. This approach has both strengths and weaknesses as Asimov seeks to increase our understanding of the quality of intelligence.*

1 What is intelligence, anyway? When I was in the Army, I received a kind of aptitude test that all soldiers took and, against a normal of 100, scored 160. No one at the base had ever seen a figure like that, and for two hours they made a big fuss over me. (It didn't mean anything. The next day I was still a buck private with KP as my highest duty.) 1

All my life I've been registering scores like that, so that I have the complacent feeling that I'm highly intelligent, and I expect other people to think so, too. Actually, though, don't such scores simply mean that I am very good at answering the type of academic questions that are considered worthy of answers by the people who make up the intelligence tests—people with intellectual bents similar to mine?

For instance, I had an auto repairman once, who, on these intelligence tests, could not possibly have scored more than 80, by my estimate. I always took it for granted that I was far more intelligent than he was. Yet, when anything went wrong with my car, I hastened to him with it, watched him anxiously as he explored its vitals, and listened to his pronouncements as though they were divine oracles—and he always fixed my car.

Well then, suppose my auto repairman devised questions for an intelligence test. Or suppose a carpenter did, or a farmer, or, indeed, almost anyone but an academician. By every one of those tests, I'd prove myself a moron. And I'd *be* a moron, too. In a world where I could not use my academic training and my verbal talents but had to do something intricate or hard, working with my hands, I would do poorly. My intelligence, then, is not absolute but is a function of the society I live in and of the fact that a small subsection of that society has managed to foist itself on the rest as an arbiter of such matters.

5 Consider my auto repairman, again. He had a habit of telling me jokes whenever he saw me. One time he raised his head from under the automobile hood to say, "Doc, a deaf-and-dumb guy went into a hardware store to ask for some nails. He put two fingers together on the counter and made hammering motions with the other hand. The clerk brought him a hammer. He shook his head and pointed to the two fingers he was hammering. The clerk brought him nails. He picked out the sizes he wanted, and left. Well, doc, the next guy who came in was a blind man. He wanted scissors. How do you suppose he asked for them?"

Indulgently, I lifted my right hand and made scissoring motions with my first two fingers. Whereupon my auto repairman laughed raucously and said, "Why, you dumb jerk, he used his *voice* and asked for them." Then he said, smugly, "I've been trying that on all my customers today." "Did you catch many?" I asked. "Quite a few," he said, "but I knew for sure I'd catch *you.*" "Why is that?" I asked. "Because you're so goddamned educated, doc, I *knew* you couldn't be very smart."

And I have an uneasy feeling he had something there.

Questions on Meaning

1. Asimov mentions both intelligence and intelligence tests, and he seems to imply that what people generally call "intelligence" is just the ability to score well on a certain kind of test. How do you respond to his statement that such tests could also be created by a carpenter or a farmer?
2. What is the difference, according to most people's thinking, between intelligence and manual dexterity? What does Asimov here imply about such a distinction?
3. Is it important to distinguish between intelligence (ability) and knowledge (learned)? Why or why not?

Questions on Rhetorical Strategy and Style

1. The repairman gives an example of what he means by "smart." See if you can find a concrete example Asimov gives of "intelligence," and comment on the significance of your finding for the success of the essay.
2. When Asimov misses the repairman's joke and gives the wrong answer, the repairman says, apparently only half-jokingly, that Asimov isn't very smart. What is the implied difference between being intelligent and being smart? Is Asimov truly saying that he isn't smart, or how else do you explain the ending line?

Writing Assignments

1. Asimov would seem to argue that there is not an absolute quality or set of abilities we can call intelligence. Do you agree with Asimov about this? Write an essay in which you define what you mean by intelligence.
2. In this essay Asimov uses the rhetorical strategy of definition to discuss intelligence. Write an essay in which you use the strategy of definition to discuss a similar abstract trait of your own choice.

From the Poets in the Kitchen

Paule Marshall

Paule Marshall (1929–) grew up in Brooklyn, NY, where she was born Paule Burke to immigrants from Barbados. She graduated from Brooklyn College in 1953 and pursued graduate studies at Hunter College. Marshall first visited Barbados when she was nine years old, and later wrote a series of poems on her impressions of her ancestral home. Primarily a fiction writer, she has published a number of short story collections and novels, including The Chosen Place *(1984),* Reena and Other Stories *(1986),* Soul Clap Hands and Sing *(1988),* Daughters *(1992),* Praisesong for the Widow *(1992), and* Brown Girl, Brownstones *(1996). Marshall's work focuses on a number of themes, particularly gender relations, white supremacy, and post-colonialism. She has received numerous awards, including a Ford Foundation Grant, a Rosenthal Award for the National Institute of Arts and Letters, and a Before Columbus Foundation American Book Award. Marshall has also lectured on Black American literature at Oxford University, Columbia University, Michigan State University, and Cornell University; she has taught creative writing at Yale University, Columbia University, the University of Massachusetts at Boston, and the University of Iowa Writers' Workshop. At present Marshall is professor emeritus of English at Virginia Commonwealth University. In this selection Marshall traces her narrative art to the women who gathered to tell stories in her mother's kitchen.*

---

1 Some years ago, when I was teaching a graduate seminar in fiction at Columbia University, a well known male novelist visited my class to speak on his development as a writer. In discussing his formative years, he didn't realize it but he seriously endangered his life by remarking that women writers are luckier than those of his sex because they usually spend so much time as children around their mothers and their mothers' friends in the kitchen.

What did he say that for? The women students immediately forgot about being in awe of him and began readying their attack for the question and answer period later on. Even I bristled. There again was that awful image of women locked away from the world in the kitchen with only each other to talk to, and their daughters locked in with them.

But my guest wasn't really being sexist or trying to be provocative or even spoiling for a fight. What he meant—when he got around to explaining himself more fully—was that, given the way children are (or were) raised in our society, with little girls kept closer to home and their mothers, the woman writer stands a better chance of being exposed, while growing up, to the kind of talk that goes on among women, more often than not in the kitchen; and that this experience gives her an edge over her male counterpart by instilling in her an appreciation for ordinary speech.

It was clear that my guest lecturer attached great importance to this, which is understandable. Common speech and the plain, workaday words that make it up are, after all, the stock in trade of some of the best fiction writers. They are the principal means by which characters in a novel or story reveal themselves and give voice sometimes to profound feelings and complex ideas about themselves and the world. Perhaps the proper measure of a writer's talent is skill in rendering everyday speech—when it is appropriate to the story—as well as the ability to tap, to exploit, the beauty, poetry and wisdom it often contains.

5 "If you say what's on your mind in the language that comes to you from your parents and your street and friends you'll probably say something beautiful." Grace Paley tells this, she says, to her students at the beginning of every writing course.

It's all a matter of exposure and a training of the ear for the would-be writer in those early years of apprenticeship. And according to my guest lecturer, this training, the best of it, often takes place in as unglamorous a setting as the kitchen.

He didn't know it, but he was essentially describing my experience as a little girl. I grew up among poets. Now they didn't look like poets—whatever that breed is supposed to look like. Nothing about them suggested that poetry was their calling. They were just a group of ordinary housewives and mothers, my mother included, who dressed in a way (shapeless housedresses, dowdy felt hats and long, dark, solemn coats) that made it impossible for me to imagine they had ever been young.

Nor did they do what poets were supposed to do—spend their days in an attic room writing verses. They never put pen to paper except to write occasionally to their relatives in Barbados. "I take my pen in hand hoping these few lines will find you in health as they leave me fair for the time being," was the way their letters invariably began. Rather, their day was spent "scrubbing floor," as they described the work they did.

Several mornings a week these unknown bards would put an apron and pair of old house shoes in a shopping bag and take the train or streetcar from our section of Brooklyn out to Flatbush. There, those who didn't have steady jobs would wait on certain designated corners for the white housewives in the neighborhood to come along and bargain with them over pay for a day's work cleaning their houses. This was the ritual even in the winter.

10 Later, armed with the few dollars they had earned, which in their vocabulary became "a few raw-mouth pennies," they made their way back to our neighborhood, where they would sometimes stop off to have a cup of tea or cocoa together before going home to cook dinner for their husbands and children.

The basement kitchen of the brownstone house where my family lived was the usual gathering place. Once inside the warm safety of its walls the women threw off the drab coats and hats, seated themselves at the large center table, drank their cups of tea or cocoa, and talked. While my sister and I sat at a smaller table over in a corner doing our homework, they talked—endlessly, passionately, poetically, and with impressive range. No subject was beyond them. True, they would indulge in the usual gossip; whose husband was running with whom, whose daughter looked slightly "in the way" (pregnant) under her bridal gown as she walked down the aisle. That sort of thing. But they also tackled the great issues of the time. They were always, for example, discussing the state of the economy. It was the mid and late 30's then, and the aftershock of the Depression, with its soup lines and suicides on Wall Street, was still being felt.

Some people, they declared, didn't know how to deal with adversity. They didn't know that you had to "tie up your belly" (hold in the pain, that is) when things got rough and go on with life. They took their image from the bellyband that is tied around the stomach of a newborn baby to keep the navel pressed in.

They talked politics. Roosevelt was their hero. He had come along and rescued the country with relief and jobs, and in gratitude they christened their sons Franklin and Delano and hoped they would live up to the names.

If F.D.R. was their hero, Marcus Garvey was their God. The name of the fiery, Jamaican-born black nationalist of the 20's was constantly invoked around the table. For he had been their leader when they first came to the United States from the West Indies shortly after World War I. They had contributed to his organization, the United Negro Improvement Association (UNIA), out of their meager salaries, bought shares in his ill-fated Black Star Shipping Line, and at the height of the movement they had marched as members of his "nurses' brigade" in their white uniforms up Seventh Avenue in Harlem during the great Garvey Day parades. Garvey: He lived on through the power of their memories.

15 And their talk was of war and rumors of wars. They raged against 15
World War II when it broke out in Europe, blaming it on the politicians. "It's these politicians. They're the ones always starting up all this lot of war. But what they care? It's the poor people got to suffer and mothers with their sons." If it was *their* sons, they swore they would keep them out of the Army by giving them soap to eat each day to make their hearts sound defective. Hitler? He was for them "the devil incarnate."

Then there was home. They reminisced often and at length about home. The old country. Barbados—or Bimshire, as they affectionately called it. The little Caribbean island in the sun they loved but had to leave. "Poor—poor but sweet" was the way they remembered it.

And naturally they discussed their adopted home. America came in for both good and bad marks. They lashed out at it for the racism they encountered. They took to task some of the people they worked for, especially those who gave them only a hard-boiled egg and a few spoonfuls of cottage cheese for lunch. "As if anybody can scrub floor on an egg and some cheese that don't have no taste to it!"

Yet although they caught H in "this man country," as they called America, it was nonetheless a place where "you could at least see your way to make a dollar." That much they acknowledged. They might even one day accumulate enough dollars, with both them and their husbands working, to buy the brownstone houses which, like my family, they were only leasing at that period. This was their consuming ambition: to "buy house" and to see the children through.

There was no way for me to understand it at the time, but the talk that filled the kitchen those afternoons was highly functional. It served as therapy, the cheapest kind available to my mother and her friends. Not only did it help them recover from the long wait on the corner that morning and the bargaining over their labor, it restored them to a sense of themselves and reaffirmed their self-worth. Through language they were able to overcome the humiliations of the work-day.

20 But more than therapy, that freewheeling, wide-ranging, exuberant talk functioned as an outlet for the tremendous creative energy they possessed. They were women in whom the need for self-expression was strong, and since language was the only vehicle readily available to them they made of it an art form that—in keeping with the African tradition in which art and life are one—was an integral part of their lives.

And their talk was a refuge. They never really ceased being baffled and overwhelmed by America—its vastness, complexity and power. Its strange customs and laws. At a level beyond words they remained fearful and in awe. Their uneasiness and fear were even reflected in their attitude toward the children they had given birth to in this country. They referred to those like myself, the little Brooklyn-born Bajans (Barbadians), as "these New York children" and complained that they couldn't discipline us properly because of the laws here. "You can't beat these children as you would like, you know, because the authorities in this place will dash you in jail for them. After all, these is New York children." Not only were we different, American, we had, as they saw it, escaped their ultimate authority.

Confronted therefore by a world they could not encompass, which ever limited their rights as parents, and at the same time finding themselves permanently separated from the world they had known, they took refuge in language. "Language is the only homeland," Czeslaw Milosz, the emigré Polish writer and Nobel Laureate, has said. This is what it became for the women at the kitchen table.

It served another purpose also, I suspect. My mother and her friends were after all the female counterpart of Ralph Ellison's invisible man. Indeed, you might say they suffered a triple invisibility, being black, female and foreigners. They really didn't count in American society except as a source of cheap labor. But given the kind of women they were, they couldn't tolerate the fact of their invisibility, their powerlessness. And they fought back, using the only weapon at their command: the spoken word.

Those late afternoon conversations on a wide range of topics were a way for them to feel they exercised some measure of control over their lives and the events that shaped them. "Soully-gal, talk yuh talk!" they were always exhorting each other. "In this man world you got to take yuh mouth and make a gun!" They were in control, if only verbally and if only for the two hours or so that they remained in our house.

For me, sitting over in the corner, being seen but not heard, which was the rule for children in those days, it wasn't only what the women talked about—the content—but the way they put things—their style. The insight, irony, wit and humor they brought to their stories and discussions and their poet's inventiveness and daring with language—which of course I could only sense but not define back then.

They had taken the standard English taught them in the primary schools of Barbados and transformed it into an idiom, an instrument that more adequately described them—changing around the syntax and imposing their own rhythm and accent so that the sentences were more pleasing to their ears. They added the few African sounds and words that had survived, such as the derisive suck-teeth sound and the word "yam," meaning to eat. And to make it more vivid, more in keeping with their expressive quality, they brought to bear a raft of metaphors, parables, Biblical quotations, sayings and the like:

"The sea ain' got no back door," they would say, meaning that it wasn't like a house where if there was a fire you could run out the back. Meaning that it was not to be trifled with. And meaning perhaps in a larger sense that man should treat all of nature with caution and respect.

"I has read hell by heart and called every generation blessed!" They sometimes went in for hyperbole.

A woman expecting a baby was never said to be pregnant. They never used that word. Rather, she was "in the way" or, better yet, "tumbling big." "Guess who I butt up on in the market the other day tumbling big again!"

And a woman with a reputation of being too free with her sexual favors was known in their book as a "thoroughfare"—the sense of men like a steady stream of cars moving up and down the road of her life. Or she might be dubbed "a free-bee," which was my favorite of the two. I liked the image it conjured up of a woman scandalous perhaps but independent, who flitted from one flower to another in a garden of male beauties, sampling their nectar, taking her pleasure at will, the roles reversed.

And nothing, no matter how beautiful, was ever described as simply beautiful. It was always "beautiful-ugly": the beautiful-ugly dress, the beautiful-ugly house, the beautiful-ugly car. Why the word "ugly," I used to wonder when the thing they were referring to was beautiful, and they knew it. Why the antonym, the contradiction, the linking of opposites? It used to puzzle me greatly as a child.

There is the theory in linguistics which states that the idiom of a people, the way they use language, reflects not only the most fundamental views they hold of themselves and the world but their very conception of reality. Perhaps in using the term "beautiful-ugly" to describe nearly everything, my mother and her friends were expressing what they believed to be a fundamental dualism in life: the idea that a thing is at the same time its opposite, and that these opposites, these contradictions make up the whole. But theirs was not a Manichaean brand of dualism that sees matter, flesh, the body, as inherently evil, because they constantly addressed each other as "soully-gal"—soul; spirit; gal: the body, flesh, the visible self. And it was clear from their tone that they gave one as much weight and importance as the other. They had never heard of the mind/body split.

As for God, they summed up His essential attitude in a phrase. "God," they would say, "don' love ugly and He ain' stuck on pretty."

Using everyday speech, the simple commonplace words—but always with imagination and skill—they gave voice to the most complex ideas. Flannery O'Connor would have approved of how they made ordinary language work, as she put it, "double-time," stretching, shading, deepening its meaning. Like Joseph Conrad they were always trying to infuse new life in the "old old words worn thin . . . by . . . careless usage." And the goals of their oral art were the same as his: "to make you hear, to make you feel . . . to make you *see.*" This was their guiding esthetic.

By the time I was 8 or 9, I graduated from the corner of the kitchen to the neighborhood library, and thus from the spoken to the written word. The Macon Street Branch of the Booklyn Public Library was an imposing half block long edifice of heavy gray masonry, with glass-paneled doors at the front and two tall metal torches symbolizing the light that comes of learning flanking the wide steps outside.

The inside was just as impressive. More steps—of pale marble with gleaming brass railings at the center and sides—led up to the circulation desk, and a great pendulum clock gazed down from the balcony stacks that faced the entrance. Usually stationed at the top of the steps like the guards outside Buckingham Palace was the custodian, a stern-faced West Indian type who for years, until I was old enough to obtain an adult card, would immediately shoo me with one hand into the Children's Room and with the other threaten me into silence, a finger to his lips. You would have thought he was the chief librarian and not just someone whose job it was to keep the brass polished and the clock wound. I put him in a story called "Barbados" years later and had terrible things happen to him at the end.

I sheltered from the storm of adolescence in the Macon Street library, reading voraciously, indiscriminately, everything from Jane Austen to Zane Grey, but with a special passion for the long, full-blown, richly detailed 18th- and 19th-century picaresque tales: "Tom Jones," "Great Expectations," "Vanity Fair."

But although I loved nearly everything I read and would enter fully into the lives of the characters—indeed, would cease being myself and become them—I sensed a lack after a time. Something I couldn't quite define was missing. And then one day browsing in the poetry section, I came across a book by someone called Paul Laurence Dunbar, and opening it I found the photograph of a wistful, sad-eyed poet who to my surprise was black. I turned to a poem at random, "Little brown-baby wif spa'klin' / eyes / Come to yo' pappy an' set on his knee." Although I had a little difficulty at first with the words in dialect, the poem spoke to me as nothing I had read before of the closeness, the special relationship I had had with my father, who by then had become an ardent believer in Father Divine and gone to live in Father's "kingdom" in Harlem. Reading it helped to ease somewhat the tight knot of sorrow and longing I carried around in my chest that refused to go away. I read another poem. "'Lias! 'Lias! Bless de Lawd! / Don' you know de day's /erbroad? / Ef you don' get up, you scamp / Dey'll be trouble in dis camp." I laughed. It reminded me of the way my mother sometimes yelled at my sister and me to get out of bed in the mornings.

And another: "Seen my lady home las' night / Jump back, honey, jump back. / Hel' huh han' an' sque'z it tight . . ." About love between a black man and a black woman. I had never seen that written about before and it roused in me all kinds of delicious feelings and hopes.

And I began to search then for books and stories and poems about "The Race" (as it was put back then), about my people. While not abandoning Thackeray, Fielding, Dickens and the others, I started asking the reference librarian, who was white, for books by Negro writers, although I must admit I did so at first with a feeling of shame—the shame I and many others used to experience in those days whenever the word "Negro" or "colored" came up.

No grade school literature teacher of mine had ever mentioned Dunbar or James Weldon Johnson or Langston Hughes. I didn't know that Zora Neale Hurston existed and was busy writing and being published during those years. Nor was I made aware of people like Frederick Douglass and Harriet Tubman—their spirit and example—or the great 19th-century abolitionist and feminist Sojourner Truth. There wasn't even Negro History Week when I attended P.S. 35 on Decatur Street!

What I needed, what all the kids—West Indian and native black American alike—with whom I grew up needed, was an equivalent of the Jewish shul, someplace where we could go after school—the schools that were shortchanging us—and read works by those like ourselves and learn about our history.

It was around that time also that I began harboring the dangerous thought of someday trying to write myself. Perhaps a poem about an apple tree, although I had never seen one. Or the story of a girl who could magically transplant herself to wherever she wanted to be in the world—such as Father Divine's kingdom in Harlem. Dunbar—his dark, eloquent face, his large volume of poems—permitted me to dream that I might someday write, and with something of the power with words my mother and her friends possessed.

When people at readings and writers' conferences ask me who my major influences were, they are sometimes a little disappointed when I don't immediately name the usual literary giants. True, I am indebted to those writers white and black, whom I read during my formative years and still read for instruction and pleasure. But they were preceded in my life by another set of giants whom I always acknowledge before all others: the group of women around the table long ago. They taught me my first lessons in the narrative art. They trained my ear. They set a standard of excellence. This is why the best of my work must be attributed to them; it stands as testimony to the rich legacy of language and culture they so freely passed on to me in the workshop of the kitchen.

Questions on Meaning

1. Why, according to Marshall, is a mastery of ordinary, everyday speech essential to the writer? How did the language of the women in her mother's kitchen belie those adjectives (ordinary, everyday)? In what ways was their language poetic?
2. In what ways was the talk in the kitchen "functional" for the women? How did both the content and the style of their talk help them to cope with their lives?
3. Why was it so important to the young Marshall to discover African-American writers? How did that discovery encourage her own aspirations? Why does she call her thoughts about becoming a writer "dangerous"?

Questions on Rhetorical Strategy and Style

1. Effective narration relies on vivid characterization. How does Marshall give life to her mother and her mother's friends? How does she portray these women, with their troubles, their triumphs, and their everyday joys? How does their language help to characterize them?
2. Marshall provides several examples of the wit and power of these women's language. Choose two or three of these examples and explain how they support her point about ordinary speech.
3. Consider Marshall's own use of language in this essay. How does her language validate her claim that the primary influence on her writing (the first cause that led to the effect) was the conversation in her mother's kitchen? Use examples to support your response.

Writing Assignments

1. Every writer, whether a famous poet or a writing student, develops in part as a result of early influences. Think of the influences on your writing—perhaps family conversations, teachers, songwriters, or other writers. Write an essay describing the impact that these people have on your writing. Focus not only on your style, but on the subjects about which you enjoy writing and the kinds of writing you lean toward.

2. Read about the major influences on one of your favorite writers; then find evidence of those influences in the writer's work. In a brief essay, discuss how those influences are reflected in the work. Use specific features of and passages from the writer in order to support your interpretation.
3. Marshall spends a good deal of time exploring the nature of the language she heard in her mother's kitchen. Think of people in your life whose language is vivid, witty, or otherwise memorable. Using examples of that speech, write an essay analyzing the impact of that language on its users and on you.

Spanglish

Janice Castro with Dan Cook and Cristina Garcia

Janice Castro was born in 1949 and lives in New York City. She has been a reporter for Time *for over twenty years and is currently a senior health care correspondent for that magazine. In 1991, she published a* Time *cover story on the health care crisis. That article, titled "Condition Critical," formed the basis of a PBS special and was endorsed by Presidents Bush and Clinton. She is the author of* The American Way of Health: How Medicine Is Changing and What It Means to You *(1994). In this selection, coauthored with Dan Cook and Cristina Garcia, Castro reports on a language called "Spanglish," a mix of Spanish and English, and, perhaps, causes us to question the definition of American English.*

1 In Manhattan a first-grader greets her visiting grandparents, hap- 1
pily exclaiming, "Come here, *siéntate!*" Her bemused grandfather, who does not speak Spanish, nevertheless knows she is asking him to sit down. A Miami personnel officer understands what a job applicant means when he says, "*Quiero un* part time." Nor do drivers miss a beat reading a billboard alongside a Los Angeles street advertising CERVEZA—SIX-PACK!

This free-form blend of Spanish and English, known as Spanglish, is common linguistic currency wherever concentrations of Hispanic Americans are found in the U.S. In Los Angeles, where 55% of the city's 3 million inhabitants speak Spanish, Spanglish is as much a part of daily life as sunglasses. Unlike the broken-English efforts of earlier immigrants from Europe, Asia and other regions, Spanglish has become a widely accepted conversational mode used casually—even

---

"Splanglish," by Janice Castro with Dan Cook and Cristina Garcia, reprinted from *Time Magazine*, July 11, 1998.

playfully—by Spanish-speaking immigrants and native-born Americans alike.

Consisting of one part Hispanicized English, one part Americanized Spanish and more than a little fractured syntax, Spanglish is a bit like a Robin Williams comedy routine: a crackling line of cross-cultural patter straight from the melting pot. Often it enters Anglo homes and families through the children, who pick it up at school or at play with their young Hispanic contemporaries. In other cases, it comes from watching TV; many an Anglo child watching *Sesame Street* has learned *uno dos tres* almost as quickly as one two three.

Spanglish takes a variety of forms, from the Southern California Anglos who bid farewell with the utterly silly "*hasta la* bye-bye" to the Cuban-American drivers in Miami who *parquean* their *carros*. Some Spanglish sentences are mostly Spanish, with a quick detour for an English word or two. A Latino friend may cut short a conversation by glancing at his watch and excusing himself with the explanation that he must "*ir al* supermarket."

5 Many of the English words transplanted in this way are simply handier than their Spanish counterparts. No matter how distasteful the subject, for example, it is still easier to say "income tax" than *impuesto sobre la renta*. At the same time, many Spanish-speaking immigrants have adopted such terms as VCR, microwave and dishwasher for what they view as largely American phenomena. Still other English words convey a cultural context that is not implicitly in the Spanish. A friend who invites you to *lonche* most likely has in mind the brisk American custom of "doing lunch" rather than the languorous afternoon break traditionally implied by *almuerzo*.

Mainstream Americans exposed to similar hybrids of German, Chinese or Hindi might be mystified. But even Anglos who speak little or no Spanish are somewhat familiar with Spanglish. Living among them, for one thing, are 19 million Hispanics. In addition, more American high school and university students sign up for Spanish than for any other foreign language.

Only in the past ten years, though, has Spanglish begun to turn into a national slang. Its popularity has grown with the explosive increases in U.S. immigration from Latin American countries. English has increasingly collided with Spanish in retail stores, offices and classrooms, in pop music and on street corners. Anglos whose ancestors picked up such Spanish words as *rancho, bronco, tornado* and *incom-*

municado, for instance, now freely use such Spanish words as *gracias, bueno, amigo* and *por favor.*

Among Latinos, Spanglish conversations often flow easily from Spanish into several sentences of English and back.

Spanglish is a sort of code for Latinos: the speakers know Spanish, but their hybrid language reflects the American culture in which they live. Many lean to shorter, clipped phrases in place of the longer, more graceful expressions their parents used. Says Leonel de la Cuesta, an assistant professor of modern languages at Florida International University in Miami: "In the U.S., time is money, and that is showing up in Spanglish as an economy of language." Conversational examples: *taipiar* (type) and *winshiwiper* (windshield wiper) replace *escribir a máquina* and *limpiaparabrisas.*

Major advertisers, eager to tap the estimated $134 billion in spending power wielded by Spanish-speaking Americans, have ventured into Spanglish to promote their products. In some cases, attempts to sprinkle Spanish through commercials have produced embarrassing gaffes. A Braniff airlines ad that sought to tell Spanish-speaking audiences they could settle back *en* (in) luxuriant *cuero* (leather) seats, for example, inadvertently said they could fly without clothes (*encuero*). A fractured translation of the Miller Lite slogan told readers the beer was "Filling, and less delicious." Similar blunders are often made by Anglos trying to impress Spanish-speaking pals. But if Latinos are amused by mangled Spanglish, they also recognize these goofs as a sort of friendly acceptance. As they might put it, *no problema.*

Questions on Meaning

1. Spanglish takes a variety of forms. What are they?
2. Spanglish is turning into a national slang. Why has its popularity grown?
3. Hispanics sometimes find Spanglish handier than English. Why?

Questions on Rhetorical Strategy and Style

1. Do the authors have an opinion about Spanglish? Do they see it as a legitimate conversational mode or are they simply reporting on its emergence? Cite specific references in the text to support your answer.
2. What statistics are used to support the emergence of Spanglish? How do those statistics support the argument?
3. The essay ends with a commentary on advertisers' use of Spanglish. Why does the essay make this shift at the end?

Writing Assignments

1. Research the English Only Amendment and write an essay in which you discuss its implications for Latinos as well as Anglos.
2. Write an essay in which you discuss Americans' attitudes about a hybrid language such as Spanglish.
3. Students are taught standard English in school while advertisers and businesses are trying to learn hybrid languages such as Spanglish to promote their products. Should hybrid languages be taught in school? Write an essay defending your position on the issue.

School vs. Education

Russell Baker

Russell Baker (1925–) was born in a rural town in Virginia and grew up in New Jersey and Maryland. He received his B. A. in English from Johns Hopkins University in 1947 and worked as a reporter for the Baltimore Sun *and then the* New York Times. *In 1962 he began writing his "Observer" column for the* Times, *which was syndicated in over 400 newspapers for more than two decades. His topics range from the mundane everyday annoyances to serious social problems, and his style is generally casual but thoughtful. In 1979 he received the Pulitzer Prize for distinguished commentary; he received the Prize again for his autobiography* Growing Up *(1982). His collections of columns and essays include* All Things Considered *(1965),* Poor Russell's Almanac *(1972),* So This is Depravity *(1980)* The Rescue of Miss Yaskell and Other Pipe Dreams *(1983), and* There's a Country in My Cellar *(1990). The following piece, first published in his* New York Times *column in 1975, intertwines serious commentary on American education and values with a spoof on what our schools teach. As you read it, think about the serious message Baker wants to communicate to us.*

1 By the age of six the average child will have completed the basic 1
American education and be ready to enter school. If the child has been attentive in these preschool years, he or she will already have mastered many skills.

From television, the child will have learned how to pick a lock, commit a fairly elaborate bank holdup, prevent wetness all day long,

---

get the laundry twice as white, and kill people with a variety of sophisticated armaments.

From watching his parents, the child, in many cases, will already know how to smoke, how much soda to mix with whiskey, what kind of language to use when angry, and how to violate the speed laws without being caught.

At this point, the child is ready for the second stage of education, which occurs in school. There, a variety of lessons may be learned in the very first days.

5 The teacher may illustrate the economic importance of belonging to a strong union by closing down the school before the child arrives. Fathers and mothers may demonstrate to the child the social cohesion that can be built on shared hatred by demonstrating their dislike for children whose pigmentation displeases them. In the latter event, the child may receive visual instruction in techniques of stoning buses, cracking skulls with a nightstick, and subduing mobs with tear gas. Formal education has begun.

During formal education, the child learns that life is for testing. This stage lasts twelve years, a period during which the child learns that success comes from telling testers what they want to hear.

Early in this stage, the child learns that he is either dumb or smart. If the teacher puts intelligent demands upon the child, the child learns he is smart. If the teacher expects little of the child, the child learns he is dumb and soon quits bothering to tell the testers what they want to hear.

At this point, education becomes more subtle. The child taught by school that he is dumb observes that neither he, she, nor any of the many children who are even dumber, ever fails to be promoted to the next grade. From this, the child learns that while everybody talks a lot about the virtue of being smart, there is very little incentive to stop being dumb.

What is the point of school, besides attendance? the child wonders. As the end of the first formal stage of education approaches, school answers this question. The point is to equip the child to enter college.

10 Children who have been taught they are smart have no difficulty. They have been happily telling testers what they want to hear for twelve years. Being artists at telling testers what they want to hear, they

are admitted to college joyously, where they promptly learn that they are the hope of America.

Children whose education has been limited to adjusting themselves to their schools' low estimates of them are admitted to less joyous colleges which, in some cases, may teach them to read.

At this stage of education, a fresh question arises for everyone. If the point of lower education was to get into college, what is the point of college? The answer is soon learned. The point of college is to prepare the student—no longer a child now—to get into graduate school. In college the student learns that it is no longer enough simply to tell the testers what they want to hear. Many are tested for graduate school; few are admitted.

Those excluded may be denied valuable certificates to prosper in medicine, at the bar, in the corporate boardroom. The student learns that the race is to the cunning and often, alas, to the unprincipled.

Thus, the student learns the importance of destroying competitors and emerges richly prepared to play his role in the great simmering melodrama of American life.

15 Afterward, the former student's destiny fulfilled, his life rich with Oriental carpets, rare porcelain, and full bank accounts, he may one day find himself with the leisure and the inclination to open a book with a curious mind, and start to become educated.

Questions on Meaning

1. What kinds of things does Baker say children learn before going to school?
2. Does Baker use any positive examples of what children learn either in or out of school? Why do you think Baker is so critical of both American society and our system of education?
3. Reread the essay's closing paragraph. Why does he say "*start* to become educated" (emphasis added)? What is different about the learning described at that moment from the schooling and lessons learned previously?

Questions on Rhetorical Strategy and Style

1. Analyze Baker's newspaper column style in this essay. What are the effects of short paragraphs, simple sentences, sweeping generalizations, and so on? How would you describe his tone?
2. Baker does not explicitly define schooling or education in a definitive way, but his meanings emerge clearly by the end of the essay. Summarize in your own words Baker's definitions of school learning and education.
3. Although Baker does not use all the rhetorical devices of persuasion in this essay, he does argue different points along the way. How does he develop his arguments that schools primarily teach one how to take tests, and that college teaches one how to succeed in a rapacious world?

Writing Assignments

1. How would you evaluate the American educational system as you have experienced it? To what extent is Baker correct in his judgment? What other statements about school and education do you think are necessary to add in order to complete a fair description of American education?
2. What does it mean to be truly educated—apart from having a college degree? Write an essay in which you define your own ideas about what education—at its best—really means.

Today's Kids Are, Like, Killing the English Language. Yeah, Right.

Kirk Johnson

Every generation, it seems, has some comment about the younger generation and the butchery it performs on the English language. Adults point to the speech of teenagers and see it as a sign of civilization in decline. School becomes the place where the problem is addressed and teenagers learn to use "proper" language, the language of grownups. In spite of these efforts, the language of youth persists, forcing us to ask the question, "What is language, anyway?" In this article from the August 9, 1998 issue of the New York Times, *Kirk Johnson offers a dynamic view of language, one in which language may be viewed as a logical and creative response to shifting social conditions, the cultural climate, and technological developments.*

1 As a father of two pre-teen boys, I have in the last year or so become a huge fan of the word "duh." This is a word much maligned by educators, linguistic brahmins and purists, but they are all quite wrong.

Duh has elegance. Duh has shades of meaning, even sophistication. Duh and its perfectly paired linguistic partner, "yeah right," are the ideal terms to usher in the millennium and the information age, and to highlight the differences from the stolid old 20th century.

Even my sons might stop me at this point and quash my hyperbole with a quickly dispensed, "Yeah, right, Dad." But hear me out:

"Today's Kids Are, Like, Killing the English Language. Yeah, Right." by Kirk Johnson, reprinted from the *New York Times*, August 9, 1998.

I have become convinced that duh and yeah right have arisen to fill a void in the language because the world has changed. Fewer questions these days can effectively be answered with yes or no, while at the same time, a tidal surge of hype and mindless blather threatens to overwhelm old-fashioned conversation. Duh and yeah right are the cure.

Good old yes and no were fine for their time—the archaic, black and white era of late industrialism that I was born into in the 1950's. The yes-or-no combo was hard and fast and most of all simple: It belonged to the Manichean red-or-dead mentality of the cold war, to manufacturing, to "Father Knows Best" and "It's a Wonderful Life."

The information-age future that my 11-year-old twins own is more complicated than yes or no. It's more subtle and supple, more loaded with content and hype and media manipulation than my childhood—or any adult's, living or dead—ever was.

And duh, whatever else it may be, is drenched with content. Between them, duh and yeah-right are capable of dividing all language and thought into an exquisitely differentiated universe. Every statement and every question can be positioned on a gray scale of understatement or overstatement, stupidity or insightfulness, information saturation or yawning emptiness.

And in an era when plain speech has become endangered by the pressures of political correctness, duh and yeah right are matchless tools of savvy, winking sarcasm and skepticism: caustic without being confrontational, incisive without being quite specific.

With duh, you can convey a response, throw in a whole basket full of auxiliary commentary about the question or the statement you're responding to, and insult the speaker all at once! As in this hypothetical exchange:

Parent: "Good morning, son, it's a beautiful day."

Eleven-year-old boy: "Duh."

And there is a kind of esthetic balance as well. Yeah—right is the yin to duh's yang, the antithesis to duh's empathetic thesis. Where duh is assertive and edgy, a perfect tool for undercutting mindless understatement or insulting repetition, yeah right is laid back, a surfer's cool kind of response to anything overwrought or oversold.

New York, for example, is duh territory, while Los Angeles is yeah—right. Television commercials can be rendered harmless and inert by simply saying, "yeah, right," upon their conclusion. Local television news reports are helped out with a sprinkling of well-placed duhs, at moments of stunning obviousness. And almost any politician's speech cries out for heaping helpings of both at various moments.

Adolescent terms like "like," by contrast, scare me to death. While I have become convinced through observation and personal experimentation that just about any adult of even modest intelligence can figure out how to use duh and yeah right properly, like is different. Like is hard. Like is, like, dangerous.

Marcel Danesi, a professor of linguistics and semiotics at the University of Toronto who has studied the language of youth and who coined the term "pubilect" to describe the dialect of pubescence, said he believes like is in fact altering the structure of the English language, making it more fluid in construction, more like Italian or some other Romance language than good old hard-and-fast Anglo-Saxon. Insert like in the middle of a sentence, he said, and a statement can be turned into a question, a question into an exclamation, an exclamation into a quiet meditation.

15 Consider these hypothetical expressions: "If you're having broccoli for dinner, Mr. Johnson, I'm, like, out of here!" and "I was, like, no way!" and perhaps most startlingly, "He was, like, duh!"

In the broccoli case, like softens the sentence. It's less harsh and confrontational than saying flatly that the serving of an unpalatable vegetable would require a fleeing of the premises.

In the second instance, like functions as a kind of a verbal quotation mark, an announcement that what follows, "no way," is to be heard differently. The quote itself can then be loaded up with any variety of intonation—irony, sarcasm, even self-deprecation—all depending on the delivery.

In the third example—"He was, like, duh!"—like becomes a crucial helping verb for duh, a verbal springboard. (Try saying the sentence without like and it becomes almost incomprehensible.)

But like and duh and yeah right, aside from their purely linguistic virtues, are also in many ways the perfect words to convey the sense of reflected reality that is part of the age we live in. Image manipulation, superficiality, and shallow media culture are, for better or worse, the backdrop of adolescent life.

20 Adults of the yes-or-no era could perhaps grow up firm in their knowledge of what things "are," but in the Age of Duh, with images reflected back from every angle at every waking moment, kids swim

in a sea of what things are "like." Distinguishing what is from what merely seems to be is a required skill of an 11-year-old today; like reflects modern life, and duh and yeah right are the tools with which such a life can be negotiated and mastered.

But there is a concealed paradox in the Age of Duh. The information overload on which it is based is built around the computer, and the computer is, of course, built around—that's right—the good old yes-or-no binary code: Billions of microcircuits all blinking on or off, black or white, current in or current out. Those computers were designed by minds schooled and steeped in the world of yes or no, and perhaps it is not too much of a stretch to imagine my sons' generation, shaped by the broader view of duh, finding another path: binary code with attitude. Besides, most computers I know already seem to have an attitude. Incorporating a little duh would at least give them a sense of humor.

Key Terms

maligned
archaic
brahmins
linguistic
stolid
dialect
hyperbole
caustic
semiotics
antithesis
self-deprecation

Questions on Meaning

1. Language is always evolving, sometimes at a rapid rate. "Duh" and "yeah right" may already be out of use. Have any terms come into the language to replace these phrases? What purpose do they serve?
2. Why does Johnson draw a distinction between the information age and the "stolid old 20th century"? How does "yeah right" signal a change in attitude?
3. Why is the information age more complicated than "yes or no"? What does Johnson mean by this?

Questions on Rhetorical Strategy and Style

1. When you first started reading this article, what did you think it was going to be about? How did Johnson surprise you or change your perception?
2. Why does Johnson quote the linguistics and semiotics professor? Why would a professor study the language of youth?
3. Johnson puts the word *like* in a different category. Why does he do this? What is different about that term?

Writing Assignments

1. Get together with a few of your classmates and put together a glossary of terms used by young people today. Think of your audience as the "stolid old" generation of people still stuck in the twentieth-century.
2. There was a time when only "standard" language was viewed as acceptable. While older people still look down on the language of youth, clearly that language has gained its own authority. Describe the examples in society that reflect the rise of youth culture

Why My Mother Can't Speak English

Garry Engkent

Born in China, Garry Engkent (1948–) escaped to Hong Kong and then, when Communist forces overtook that country, to Ontario. He learned English quickly, both from schooling and from frequent trips to the movies. In 1980 Engkent received a Ph.D. in English from the University of Ottawa, and has since taught at several universities. He currently teaches literature and writing at both Seneca College and Ryerson University. A prolific writer, Engkent's short stories have been published widely. His work often focuses on the clash of cultures experienced by immigrants, particularly those from China; that cultural clash is felt within the family as well, as children become acculturated while their parents (particularly their mothers) cling to Chinese values. In this essay Engkent draws from memory and embellishes with fiction the story of why and how his mother finally became a Canadian citizen.

1 My mother is seventy years old. Widowed for five years now, 1
she lives alone in her own house except for the occasions when I come home to tidy her household affairs. She has been in *gum san,* the golden mountain, for the past thirty years. She clings to the old-country ways so much so that today she astonishes me with this announcement:

"I want to get my citizenship," she says as she slaps down the *Dai Pao,* "before they come and take away my house."

"Nobody's going to do that. This is Canada."

"So everyone says," she retorts, "but did you read what the *Dai Pao* said? Ah, you can't read Chinese. The government is cutting back on old-age pensions. Anybody who hasn't got citizenship will lose everything. Or worse."

The *Dai Pao* can't even typeset accurately," I tell her. Sometimes I worry about the information Mother receives from that biweekly community newspaper. "Don't worry—the Ministry of Immigration won't send you back to China."

"Little you know," she snaps back. "I am old, helpless, and without citizenship. Reasons enough. Now, get me citizenship. Hurry!"

"Mother, getting citizenship papers is not like going to the bank to cash in your pension cheque. First, you have to—"

"Excuses, my son, excuses. When your father was alive—"

"Oh, Mother, not again! You throw that at me every—"

"—made excuses, too." Her jaw tightens. "If you can't do this little thing for your own mother, well, I will just have to go and beg your cousin to . . ."

Everytime I try to explain about the ways of the *fan gwei,* she thinks I do not want to help her. "I'll do it, I'll do it, okay? Just give me some time."

"That's easy for you," Mother snorts. "You're not seventy years old. You're not going to lose your pension. You're not going to lose your house. Now, how much *lai-shi* will this take?"

After all these years in *gum san* she cannot understand that you don't give government officials *lai-shi,* the traditional Chinese money gift to persons who do things for you.

"That won't be necessary," I tell her, "and you needn't go to my cousin."

Mother picks up the *Dai Pao* again and says: "Why should I beg at the door of a village cousin when I have a son who is a university graduate?"

I wish my father were alive. Then he would be doing this. But he is not here, and as a dutiful son, I am responsible for the welfare of my widowed mother. So I take her to Citizenship Court.

There are several people from the Chinese community waiting there. Mother knows a few of the Chinese women and she chats with them. My cousin is there too.

"I thought your mother already got her citizenship," he says to me. "Didn't your father—"

"No, he didn't."

He shakes his head sadly. "Still, better now than never. That's why I'm getting these people through."

"So they've been reading the *Dai Pao.*"

He gives me a quizzical look, so I explain to him, and he laughs.

"You are the new generation," he says. "You didn't live long enough in *hon san,* the sweet land, to understand the fears of the old. You can't expect the elderly to renounce all attachments to China for the ways of the *fan gwei,* white devils. How old is she, seventy now? Much harder."

"She woke me up this morning at six and Citizenship Court doesn't open till ten."

The doors of the court finally open, and Mother motions me to hurry. We wait in line for a while.

The clerk distributes applications and tells me the requirements. Mother wants to know what the clerk is saying, so half the time I translate for her.

The clerk suggests that we see one of the liaison officers.

"Your mother has been living in Canada for the past thirty years and she still can't speak English?"

"It happens," I tell the liaison officer.

"I find it hard to believe that—not one word?"

"Well, she understands some restaurant English," I tell her. "You know, French fries, pork chops, soup, and so on. And she can say a few words."

"But will she be able to understand the judge's questions? The interview with the judge, as you know, is an important part of the citizenship procedure. Can she read the booklet? What does she know about Canada?"

"So you don't think my mother has a chance?"

"The requirements are that the candidate must be able to speak either French or English, the two official languages of Canada. The candidate must be able to pass an oral interview with the citizenship judge, and then he or she must be able to recite the oath of allegiance—"

"My mother needs to speak English," I conclude for her.

"Look, I don't mean to be rude, but why didn't your mother learn English when she first came over?"

I have not been translating this conversation, and Mother, annoyed and agitated, asks me what is going on. I tell her there is a slight problem.

"What problem?" Mother opens her purse, and I see her taking a small red envelope—*lai shi*—I quickly cover her hand.

"What's going on?" the liaison officer demands.

"Nothing," I say hurriedly. "Just a cultural misunderstanding, I assure you."

My mother rattles off some indignant words, and I snap back in Chinese: "Put that away! The woman won't understand, and we'll be in a lot of trouble."

The officer looks confused, and I realize that an explanation is needed.

"My mother was about to give you a money gift as a token of appreciation for what you are doing for us. I was afraid you might misconstrue it as a bribe. We have no intention of doing that."

"I'm relieved to hear it."

We conclude the interview, and I take Mother home. Still clutching the application, Mother scowls at me.

"I didn't get my citizenship papers. Now I will lose my old-age pension. The government will ship me back to China. My old bones will lie there while your father's will be here. What will happen to me?"

How can I teach her to speak the language when she is too old to learn, too old to want to learn? She resists anything that is *fan gwei.* She does everything the Chinese way. Mother spends much time staring blankly at the four walls of her house. She does not cry. She sighs and shakes her head. Sometimes she goes about the house touching her favourite things.

"This is all your dead father's fault," she says quietly. She turns to the photograph of my father on the mantel. Daily, she burns incense, pours fresh cups of fragrant tea, and spreads dishes of his favourite fruits in front of the framed picture as is the custom. In memory of his passing, she treks two miles to the cemetery to place flowers by his headstone, to burn ceremonial paper money, and to talk to him. Regularly, rain or shine, or even snow, she does these things. Such love, such devotion, now such vehemence. Mother curses my father, her husband, in his grave.

When my mother and I emigrated from China, she was forty years old, and I, five. My father was already a well-established restaurant owner. He put me in school and Mother in the restaurant kitchen, washing dishes and cooking strange foods like hot dogs, hamburgers, and French fries. She worked seven days a week from six in the morning until eleven at night. This lasted for twenty-five years, almost to the day of my father's death.

50 The years were hard on her. The black-and-white photographs show a robust woman; now I see a withered, frail, white-haired old woman, angry, frustrated with the years, and scared of losing what little material wealth she has to show for the toil in *gum san.*

"I begged him," Mother says. "But he would either ignore my pleas or say: 'What do you need to know English for? You're better off here in the kitchen. Here you can talk to the others in our own tongue. English is far too complicated for you. How old are you now? Too old to learn a new language. Let the young speak *fan gwei.* All you need is to understand the orders from the waitresses. Anyway, if you need to know something, the men will translate for you. I am here; I can do your talking for you.' "

As a conscientious boss of the young male immigrants, my father would force them out of the kitchen and into the dining room. "The kitchen is no place for you to learn English. All you do is speak Chinese in here. To survive in *gum san,* you have to speak English, and the only way you can do that is to wait on tables and force yourselves to speak English with the customers. How can you get your families over here if you can't talk to the immigration officers in English?"

A few of the husbands who had the good fortune to bring their wives over to Canada hired a retired school teacher to teach a bit of English to their wives. Father discouraged Mother from going to those once-a-week sessions.

"That old woman will get rich doing nothing. What have these women learned? *Fan gwei* ways—make-up lipstick, smelly perfumes, fancy clothes. Once she gets through with them, they won't be Chinese women any more—and they certainly won't be white either."

55 Some of the husbands heeded the words of the boss, for he was older than they, and he had been in the white devil's land longer. These wives stayed home and tended the children, or they worked in the restaurant kitchen, washing dishes and cooking *fan gwei* foods, and talking in Chinese about the land and the life they had been forced to leave behind.

"He was afraid that I would leave him. I depended on him for everything. I could not go anywhere by myself. He drove me to work and he drove me home. He only taught me how to print my name so that I could sign anything he wanted me to, bank cheques, legal documents . . ."

Perhaps I am not Chinese enough any more to understand why my mother would want to take in the sorrow, the pain, and the anguish, and then to recount them every so often.

Once, I was presumptuous enough to ask her why she would want to remember in such detail. She said that the memories didn't hurt any more. I did not tell her that her reminiscences cut me to the quick. Her only solace now is to be listened to.

My father wanted more sons, but she was too old to give him more. One son was not enough security he needed for old age. "You smell of stale perfume," she would say to him after he had driven the waitresses home. Or, to me, she would say: "A second mother will not treat you so well, you know," and, "Would you like another mother at home?" Even at that tender age, I knew that in China a husband could take a second wife. I told her that I didn't need another mother, and she would nod her head.

60 When my father died five years ago, she cried and cried. "Don't leave me in this world. Let me die with you."

Grief-stricken, she would not eat for days. She was so weak from hunger that I feared she wouldn't be able to attend the funeral. At his grave side, she chanted over and over a dirge, commending his spirit to the next world and begging the goddess of mercy to be kind to him. By custom, she set his picture on the mantel and burned incense in front of it daily. And we would go to the cemetery often. There she would arrange fresh flowers and talk to him in the gentlest way.

Often she would warn me: "The world of the golden mountain is so strange, *fan gwei* improprieties, and customs. The white devils will have you abandon your own aged mother to some old-age home to rot away and die unmourned. If you are here long enough, they will turn your head until you don't know who you are—Chinese."

My mother would convert the months and the days into the Chinese lunar calendar. She would tell me about the seasons and the harvests and the festivals in China. We did not celebrate any *fan gwei* holidays.

My mother sits here at the table, fingering the booklet from the Citizenship Court. For thirty-some years, my mother did not learn the English language, not because she was not smart enough, not because she was too old to learn, and not because my father forbade her, but because she feared that learning English would change her Chinese soul. She only learned enough English to survive in the restaurant kitchen.

65 Now, Mother wants *gum san* citizenship.

"Is there no hope that I will be given it?" she asks.

"There's always a chance," I tell her. "I'll hand in the application."

"I should have given that person the *lai-shi,*" Mother says obstinately.

"Maybe I should teach you some English," I retort. "You have about six months before the oral interview."

70 "I am seventy years old," she says. "*Lai shi* is definitely much easier."

My brief glimpse into Mother's heart is over, and it has taken so long to come about. I do not know whether I understand my aged mother any better now. Despite my mother's constant instruction, there is too much *fan gwei* in me.

The booklet from the Citizenship Court lies, unmoved, on the table, gathering dust for weeks. She has not mentioned citizenship again with the urgency of that particular time. Once in a while, she would say: "They have forgotten me. I told you they don't want old Chinese women as citizens."

Finally, her interview date is set. I try to teach her some ready-made phrases, but she forgets them.

"You should not sigh so much. It is bad for your health," Mother observes.

75 On the day of her examination, I accompany her into the judge's chamber. I am more nervous than my mother.

Staring at the judge, my mother remarks: "*Noi yren.*" The judge shows interest in what my mother says, and I translate it: "She says you're a woman."

The judge smiles. "Yes. Is that strange?"

"If she is going to examine me," Mother tells me, "I might as well start packing for China. Sell my house. Dig up your father's bones, and I'll take them back with me."

Without knowing what my mother said, the judge reassures her. "This is just a formality. Really. We know that you obviously want to be part of our Canadian society. Why else would you go through all this trouble? We want to welcome you as a new citizen, no matter what race, nationality, religion, or age. And we want you to be proud—as a new Canadian."

80 Six weeks have passed since the interview with the judge. Mother receives a registered letter telling her to come in three weeks' time to take part in the oath of allegiance ceremony.

With patient help from the same judge, my mother recites the oath and becomes a Canadian citizen after thirty years in *gum san.*

"How does it feel to be a Canadian?" I ask.

"In China, this is the eighth month, the season of harvest." Then she adds: "The *Dai Pao* says that the old-age pension cheques will be increased by nine dollars next month."

As we walk home on this bright autumn morning, my mother clutches her piece of paper. Citizenship. She says she will go up to the cemetery and talk to my father this afternoon. She has something to tell him.

Questions on Meaning

1. Why did the author's father refuse to allow his wife to learn English? How does the author suggest that his mother, at least at some level of consciousness, agreed with this reasoning?
2. What is the significance of the widow's mourning rituals for her dead husband? How do these rituals help readers to understand Engkent's mother?
3. How does the judge interpret Mrs. Engkent's determination to be a Canadian citizen? What does this misperception suggest about other immigrants' motivations for citizenship?

Questions on Strategy and Style

1. Engkent chooses to deliver his narrative in the present tense. How does this choice affect the impact of his story? How would the story have been changed had he used the more traditional past tense?
2. What have been the effects of not having learned English for the author's mother? In what ways do these effects seem to have been positive? In what ways negative?
3. Engkent presents a number of contrasts in this story: ways of dealing with Canadian as opposed to Chinese bureaucracy, men's and women's roles in Chinese culture, and his mother's devotion to and resentment of her husband, among others. Choose one significant contrast in the narrative and explain how it serves the author's purpose in relating his mother's story.

Writing Assignments

1 Current discussions of multiculturalism often focus on the extent to which immigrants should attempt to retain their home culture. Write an essay explaining your position on the value of maintaining one's ethnic identity.
2. Engkent's narrative explores generational differences in addition to cultural differences between mother and son. Write a story about an incident in your life in which you became aware of generational differences between you and your grandparents, parents, or other older members of the family.
3. Read several historical accounts of Chinese immigration to Canada, and write a report chronicling the experience. Focus on such issues as learning English or French, finding employment, overcoming discrimination, and raising children in Canadian culture.

Writing Is my Passion

bell hooks

bell hooks (1952–), the pseudonym of Gloria Watkins, was born in Kentucky. She received a B.A. from Stanford University and a Ph.D. from the University of California, Santa Cruz. An advocate for African-American women in the feminist movement as well as a critic of the white male–dominated U.S. power structure, hooks has taught at Oberlin College and Yale University. Her books include Ain't I a Woman: Black Women and Feminism *(1981),* Feminist Theory: From Margin to Center *(1984),* Talking Back: Thinking Feminist, Thinking Black *(1989),* Yearning: Race, Gender, and Cultural Politics *(1990),* Breaking Bread: Insurgent Black Intellectual Life *(1992),* Black Looks: Race and Representation *(1992),* Outlaw Culture *(1994),* Teaching to Transgress: Education as the Practice of Freedom *(1994),* Reel to Real: Race, Sex, and Class at the Movies *(1996),* and Remembering Rapture *(1999). The following selection is a chapter from* Wounds of Passion: A Writing Life *(1997).*

1 Writing is my passion. Words are the way to know ecstasy. 1
Without them life is barren. The poet insists *Language is a body of suffering and when you take up language you take up the suffering too.* All my life I have been suffering for words. Words have been the source of the pain and the way to heal.

Struck as a child for talking, for speaking out of turn, for being out of my place. Struck as a grown woman for not knowing when to shut up, for not being willing to sacrifice words for desire. Struck by writing a book that disrupts. There are many ways to be hit. Pain is the price we pay to speak the truth. *Language is a body of suffering and when you take up language you take up the suffering too.*

Nothing is as simple as it seems, so much is neither good nor bad, but always a blend of truths. In the household of my childhood, that place where I was held prisoner, there was no doubt in anyone's mind that I would write, that I would become a writer, magician of words, one who suffers well. *She works hard in the name of love. She who is able to sacrifice.*

Nothing is as simple as it seems. No one in the house of my childhood doubts my power to create. I learn doubt when I leave home I learn to doubt my intelligence, my creativity in the integrated world—at college and in the arms of talented men. They try and teach me to fear a woman's word, to doubt whether her words can ever be as good, as perfect as any man's sound. No wonder then there is something in me that clings to childhood—to the girl who loved Emily Dickinson, writer, thinker, dreamer of worlds. In the shadow of her presence, I am without doubt. I know I can become a writer.

5 *She stayed with him much longer than she should have. Her staying was* 5
never a way to cling to love. She feared losing the discipline to write. She entered a committed relationship so soon, so young devote herself to writing. So much in the world distracted her from words. So much made life seem crazy. At times she dreamed of returning home. Despite all the madness of home, she had always found a place to read, contemplate life, and write there.

She is right. Nothing is as simple as it seems. You would think all those fancy colleges she went to so far away from home would have made it easy to write. Baba used to asked her How can you live so far away from your people. At home she doubted her capacity to love, to be intimate, to make friends even. Introverted and awkward she doubted so much about herself but never her ability to imagine, to write.

No one really says how it will be. When we try to leave behind all the limits of race and gender and class, to transcend them, to get to the heart of the matter. No one really says how painful it will be—that just when you think you are moving forward in life some new thing, another barrier surfaces that just stops you in your tracks. For all that goes wrong in my life with Mack, I have had shelter here, a sanctuary for that part of me that was destined to write, to make a life in words.

Language is a body of suffering and when you take up language you take up the suffering too.

Nobody ever talked to us about how we would become these new women and men transformed by feminist movement. All the cultural revolutions created by black liberation and sexual liberation and women's liberation, and yet there is still no map—nothing that will guide us safely to mutual love and respect. We lose our way. One thing is certain—we can never turn back.

After all our feminist victory, there is still a grave silence about the issue of whether women can be in love relationships with men and truly develop as writers. I believe my relationship with Mack strengthens me as a thinker and a writer. I used to say that we were better at giving each other the space to be independent than we were at being together. I grew stronger as a writer at all times, even during times when we were in crisis. Writing was my refuge and my rescue.

She believed for so long that if she left their relationship she might cease to write. After all she became a disciplined published writer there in the shadows of their love. To depart from that love might mean to depart from writing. She could imagine living without him. She could not imagine living without words. And so she remained.

They all wanted to know *Why did you stay with him so long.* I am weary explaining. Doesn't everyone realize that nothing is as simple as it seems. Our relationship falling apart is no one's fault. Everybody wants somebody to blame. I wanted to make sense of the pain. The ways I was hurt in this relationship and the ways I hurt were only one fragment of a larger piece. When I left home, I thought I was leaving hurt behind. I did not even imagine that there were ways to be hurt in the world outside home. When you are confined to a small segregated area across the tracks, away from so much going on in the larger world, innocence is still possible. Measured against the pain in the world, home seemed a safe haven, both the home I left and the home I had made with Mack.

To explain things she says: Every terrorist regime in the world uses isolation to break the human spirit. It is not difficult for her to see that women writers, especially black women writers, are isolated. She can count the ones whose work is recognized. She can see for herself how many die alone, unloved, their work forgotten. She can see for herself how many remain invisible. She can see how many go mad.

Haunted by the fear of madness, I am deeply convinced that the world is not a safe place for me. I remain reluctant to move, to change, to go anywhere. I need company to move outside the home. That was the way it was growing up. A girl was never left alone. When I came to college I realized I had never been alone not even for a day. Whenever we left the house as girls we were escorted. In private I love to be alone. In public I prefer company.

They were always so together the two of them. They did everything together. No wonder then it was surprising that they could not work together in the same room. In private they were alone, they were silent. In private they were devoted to work.

Women sacrifice for words. They suffer and they die. The poet Audre Lorde visits our house. She sits and flirts on our Victorian deep red couch. She has just autographed a copy of my favorite poem "Litany for Survival." Her words say everything there is to say about the perils the exploited and the oppressed face coming to voice. She goes straight to the heart of the matter: *When we are loved we are afraid love will vanish / when we are alone we are afraid love will never return / and when we speak we are afraid our words will not be heard not welcome / but when we are silent we are still afraid.*

Questions on Meaning

1. "Nothing is as simple as it seems, so much is neither good nor bad, but always a blend of truths." How do you respond to this statement? Discuss instances in your life where this seems true. Why does the author believe this?
2. Sometimes we are able to tell when a person is destined to do some particular thing in life. In this author's case, what characteristics does she possess that leads readers to predict that she will be a writer?
3. In this selection, the author refers to the major cultural movements of black, sexual, and women's liberation. Speculate on why the author feels these movements have not guided us "safely to mutual love and respect." Draw on your own observations and experiences.

Questions on Rhetorical Strategy and Style

1. One noticeable device in this selection is the shift in voice that occurs in the italics. What is the purpose of this device? What kind of information do these passages contain?
2. There are moments in the text where the author repeats sentence patterns and even whole statements. Locate a few such examples and explain how they affect the tone of the essay and the "Questions on Meaning" they convey. Also, she makes use of sentence fragments to create an effect. Discuss these, as well.
3. In the phrase "Language is a body of suffering . . . ," the word *body* takes on metaphoric significance. How do writing and the body relate to one another, according to the author?

Writing Assignments

1. To be passionate about something is to identify it as central to one's life. Without it, we would be the same. For hooks, writing is her passion. Without it life would be far less meaningful. Any one of us could have the same feeling, in varying degrees of intensity. Explore this feeling in an essay of your own. What one thing do you feel passionate about? In what ways is it essential to your sense of self?

2. This is an example of a literacy narrative. Many such essays discuss the struggles involved in gaining new knowledge and awareness. It can be true that in the process of moving forward one must also leave something behind. In other words, to progress, one must sacrifice. Explore this concept in a personal essay. To what extent is this true for you?

The Joy and Enthusiasm of Reading

Rick Moody

Rick Moody (1961–) is the author of such novels as Purple America *(1997),* The Ice Storm *(1994),* Garden State *(1992), and short story collections,* Demonology *(2001) and* The Ring of Brightest Angels Around Heaven *(1995). In 2002 he published a memoir entitled* The Black Veil, *in which he describes a life and subsequent breakdown that led him to a psychiatric hospital in New York. He has won numerous awards for his writing, most notably a Pushcart Prize and a Guggenheim fellowship. Moody was born in Brooklyn and currently lives in New York. He describes his love of books in this radio essay from the National Public Radio series "This I Believe."*

1 I believe in the absolute and unlimited liberty of reading. I believe 1
in wandering through the stacks and picking out the first thing that strikes me. I believe in choosing books based on the dust jacket. I believe in reading books because others dislike them or find them dangerous. I believe in choosing the hardest book imaginable. I believe in reading up on what others have to say about this difficult book, and then making up my own mind.

Part of this has to do with Mr. Buxton, who taught me Shakespeare in 10th grade. We were reading *Macbeth.* Mr. Buxton, who probably had better things to do, nonetheless agreed to meet one night to go over the text line by line. The first thing he did was point out the repetition of motifs. For example, the reversals of things ("fair is foul and foul is fair"). Then there was the unsexing of Lady Macbeth and the association in the play of masculinity with violence.

What Mr. Buxton didn't tell me was what the play *meant.* He left the conclusions to me. The situation was much the same with my religious studies teacher in 11th grade, Mr. Flanders, who encouraged me to have my own relationship with the Gospels, and perhaps he quoted Jesus of Nazareth in the process. "Therefore speak I to them in parables: Because they seeing, see not; and hearing they hear not, neither do they understand."

High school was followed by college, where I read Umberto Eco's *Role of the Reader,* in which it is said that the reader completes the text, that the text is never finished until it meets this voracious and engaged reader. The open texts, Eco calls them. In college, I read some of the great Europeans and Latin Americans: Borges and Kafka, Genet and Beckett, Artaud, Proust — open texts all. I may not have known *why* Kafka's *Metamorphosis* is about a guy who turns into a bug, but I knew that some said cockroach, and others, European dung beetle.

5 There are those critics, of course, who insist that there are right ways and wrong ways to read every book. No doubt they arrived at these beliefs through their own adventures in the stacks. And these are important questions for philosophers of every stripe. And yet I know only what joy and enthusiasm about reading have taught me, in bookstores new and used.

I believe there is not now and never will be an authority who can tell me how to interpret, how to read, how to find the pearl of literary meaning in all cases. Nietzsche says, "Supposing truth is a woman — what then?" Supposing the truth is not hard, fast, masculine, simple, direct? You could spend a lifetime thinking about this sentence, and making it your own. In just this way, I believe in the freedom to see literature, history, truth, unfolding ahead of me like a book whose spine has just now been cracked.

Questions on Meaning

1. Why does the author want to read certain books, "because others dislike them or find them dangerous"?
2. What did Mr. Buxton teach Moody about reading and literature?
3. What is significant about "the reversal of things" as it pertains to Moody's main point?

Questions on Rhetorical Strategy and Style

1. Why does the author include in his essay stories about two of his teachers? How does he expect listeners to respond?
2. Where does Moody reveal his main idea or thesis? In which parts of the essay is his sense of joy most revealed?

Writing Assignments

1. Moody's essay is an example of what is called a literacy narrative, that is, a story of how one came to be a particular literate person. Write your own literacy narrative. Define literacy in any way relevant to you and describe the influences and events that form the basis of your story.
2. Write an essay about the teacher who had the greatest influence on you. Why did he or she have such an effect on you? Did you have any conflicts with this teacher? Was he or she necessarily your favorite teacher?

Silence

Maxine Hong Kingston

Maxine Hong Kingston (1940–) was born in Stockton, California. One of eight children—two born in China, Kingston and the others born in the United States—Kingston spent her youth with many Chinese immigrants. Her first language was Chinese, and she was exposed from birth to the rich oral traditions of Chinese culture. Kingston entered the University of California at Berkeley on scholarship as an engineering major, but quickly switched to English literature. She received a B. A. (1962) and a teaching certificate (1965) and spent many years teaching in Hawaii. The recipient of both the National Book Critics Circle Award and the American Book Award, Kingston has written widely on life as a Chinese-American. Her books include The Woman Warrior: Memoirs of a Girlhood Among Ghosts *(1976),* China Men (1980), and Tripmaster Monkey: His Fake Book *(1989). Kingston's works are imbued with Chinese culture and reflect the rhythm of Chinese-American speech. In this essay, Kingston contrasts her years of silence in American school with the sounds of her Chinese school, as she reveals how language and cultural differences impacted her early years.*

1 When I went to kindergarten and had to speak English for 1
the first time, I became silent. A dumbness—a shame—still cracks my voice in two, even when I want to say "hello" casually, or ask an easy question in front of the check-out counter, or ask directions of a bus driver. I stand frozen, or I hold up the line with the complete, grammatical sentence that comes squeaking out at impossible length. "What did you say?" says the cab driver, or "Speak

From *The Woman Warrior* by Maxine Hong Kingston. Published by Alfred A. Knopf, Inc.

up," so I have to perform again, only weaker the second time. A telephone call makes my throat bleed and takes up that day's courage. It spoils my day with self-disgust when I hear my broken voice come skittering out into the open. It makes people wince to hear it, I'm getting better, though. Recently I asked the postman for special-issue stamps; I've waited since childhood for postmen to give me some of their own accord. I am making progress, a little every day.

My silence was thickest—total—during the three years that I covered my school paintings with black paint. I painted layers of black over houses and flowers and suns, and when I drew on the blackboard, I put a layer of chalk on top. I was making a stage curtain, and it was the moment before the curtain parted or rose. The teachers called my parents to school, and I saw they had been saving my pictures, curling and cracking, all alike and black. The teachers pointed to the pictures and looked serious, talked seriously too, but my parents did not understand English. ("The parents and teachers of criminals were executed," said my father.) My parents took the pictures home. I spread them out (so black and full of possibilities) and pretended the curtains were swinging open, flying up, one after another, sunlight underneath, mighty operas.

During the first silent year I spoke to no one at school, did not ask before going to the lavatory, and flunked kindergarten. My sister also said nothing for three years, silent in the playground and silent at lunch. There were other quiet Chinese girls not of our family, but most of them got over it sooner than we did. I enjoyed the silence. At first it did not occur to me I was supposed to talk or to pass kindergarten. I talked at home and to one or two of the Chinese kids in class. I made motions and even made some jokes. I drank out of a toy saucer when the water spilled out of the cup, and everybody laughed, pointing at me, so I did it some more. I didn't know that Americans don't drink out of saucers.

I liked the Negro students (Black Ghosts) best because they laughed the loudest and talked to me as if I were a daring talker too. One of the Negro girls had her mother coil braids over her ears Shanghai-style like mine; we were Shanghai twins except that she was covered with black like my paintings. Two Negro kids enrolled in Chinese school, and the teachers gave them Chinese names. Some Negro kids walked me to school and home, protecting me from the Japanese kids, who hit me and chased me and stuck gum in my ears. The Japanese kids were noisy and tough. They appeared one day in kindergarten, released from concentration camp, which was a tic-tac-toe mark, like barbed wire, on the map.

It was when I found out I had to talk that school become a misery, that the silence became a misery. I did not speak and felt bad each time that I did not speak. I read aloud in first grade, though, and heard the barest whisper with little squeaks come out of my throat. "Louder," said the teacher, who scared the voice away again. The other Chinese girls did not talk either, so I knew the silence had to do with being a Chinese girl.

Reading out loud was easier than speaking because we did not have to make up what to say, but I stopped often, and the teacher would think I'd gone quiet again. I could not understand "I." The Chinese "I" has seven strokes, intricacies. How could the American "I," assuredly wearing a hat like the Chinese, have only three strokes, the middle so straight? Was it out of politeness that this writer left off the strokes the way a Chinese has to write her own name small and crooked? No, it was not politeness; "I" is a capital and "you" is lower-case. I stared at that middle line and waited so long for its black center to resolve into tight strokes and dots that I forgot to pronounce it. The other troublesome word was "here," no strong consonant to hang on to, and so flat, when "here" is two mountainous ideographs. The teacher, who had already told me every day how to read "I" and "here," put me in the low corner under the stairs again, where the noisy boys usually sat.

When my second grade class did a play, the whole class went to the auditorium except the Chinese girls. The teacher, lovely and Hawaiian, should have understood about us, but instead left us behind in the classroom. Our voices were too soft or nonexistent, and our parents never signed the permission slips anyway. They never signed anything unnecessary. We opened the door a crack and peeked out, but closed it again quickly. One of us (not me) won every spelling bee, though.

I remember telling the Hawaiian teacher, "We Chinese can't sing 'land where our fathers died.' " She argued with me about politics, while I meant because of curses. But how can I have that memory when I couldn't talk? My mother says that we, like the ghosts, have no memories.

After American school, we picked up our cigar boxes, in which we had arranged books, brushes, and an inkbox neatly, and went to

Chinese school, from 5:00 to 7:30 P.M. There we changed together, voices rising and failing, loud and soft, some boys shouting, everybody reading together, reciting together and not alone with one voice. When we had a memorization test, the teacher let each of us come to his desk and say the lesson to him privately, while the rest of the class practiced copying or tracing. Most of the teachers were men. The boys who were so well behaved in the American school played tricks on them and talked back to them. The girls were not mute. They screamed and yelled during recess, when there were no rules; they had fistfights. Nobody was afraid of children hurting themselves or of children hurting school property. The glass doors to the red and green balconies with the gold joy symbols were left wide open so that we could run out and climb the fire escapes. We played capture-the-flag in the auditorium, where Sun Yat-sen and Chiang Kai-shek's pictures hung at the back of the stage, the Chinese flag on their left and the American flag on their right. We climbed the teak ceremonial chairs and made flying leaps off the stage. One flag headquarters was behind the glass door and the other on stage right. Our feet drummed on the hollow stage. During recess the teachers locked themselves up in their office with the shelves of books, copybooks, inks from China. They drank tea and warmed their hands at a stove. There was no play supervision. At recess we had the school to ourselves, and also we could roam as far as we could go—downtown, Chinatown stores, home—as long as we returned before the bell rang.

10 At exactly 7:30 the teacher again picked up the brass bell that sat on his desk and swung it over our heads, while we charged down the stairs, our cheering magnified in the stairwell. Nobody had to line up.

Not all of the children who were silent at American school found voice at Chinese school. One new teacher said each of us had to get up and recite in front of the class, who was to listen. My sister and I had memorized the lesson perfectly. We said it to each other at home, one chanting, one listening. The teacher called on my sister to recite first. It was the first time a teacher had called on the second-born to go first. My sister was scared. She glanced at me and looked away; I looked down at my desk. I hoped that she could do it because if she could, then I would have to. She opened her mouth and a voice came out that wasn't a whisper, but it wasn't a proper voice either. I hoped that she would not cry, fear breaking up her voice like twigs underfoot. She sounded as if she were trying to sing through weeping and strangling. She did not pause or stop to end the embarrassment. She kept going until she said the last word, and then she sat down. When it was my turn, the same voice came out, a crippled animal running on broken legs. You could hear splinters in my voice, bones rubbing jagged against one another. I was loud, though. I was glad I didn't whisper.

How strange that the emigrant villagers are shouters, hollering face to face. My father asks, "Why is it I can hear Chinese from blocks away? Is it that I understand the language? Or is it they talk loud?" They turn the radio up full blast to hear the operas, which do not seem to hurt their ears. And they yell over the singers that wail over the drums, everybody talking at once, big arm gestures, spit flying. You can see the disgust on American faces looking at women like that. It isn't just the loudness. It is the way Chinese sounds, ching-chong ugly, to American ears, not beautiful like Japanese sayonara words with the consonants and vowels as regular as Italian. We make guttural peasant noise and have Ton Duc Thang names you can't remember. And the Chinese can't hear Americans at all; the language is too soft and western music unbearable. I've watched a Chinese audience laugh, visit, talk-story, and holler during a piano recital, as if the musician could not hear them. A Chinese-American, somebody's son, was playing Chopin, which has no punctuation, no cymbals, no gongs. Chinese piano music is five black keys. Normal Chinese women's voices are strong and bossy. We American-Chinese girls had to whisper to make ourselves American-feminine. Apparently we whispered even more softly than the Americans. Once a year the teachers referred my sister and me to speech therapy, but our voices would straighten out, unpredictably normal, for the therapists. Some of us gave up, shook our heads, and said nothing, not one word. Some of us could not even shake our heads. At times shaking my head no is more self-assertion than I can manage. Most of us eventually found some voice, however faltering. We invented an American-feminine speaking personality.

Key Terms

skittering
intricacies
assuredly
resolve
consonant
ideographs
ceremonial
emigrant
guttural
faltering

Questions on Meaning

1. Why does Kingston enjoy silence when she first attends American School? What makes her silence "a misery"?
2. What are Kingston's reactions to the English "I"? Why does she consider the English "I" and "you" impolite?
3. According to Kingston, why do Americans dislike hearing Chinese spoken? Why do Chinese people have difficulty hearing the American language?

Questions on Rhetorical Strategy and Style

1. Kingston uses a number of comparisons and contrasts in this essay. Make a list of the differences between Chinese and American schools, and the Chinese and American languages. How do these contrasts emphasize cultural differences?
2. Kingston uses several examples of her behavior to illustrate her point about growing up Chinese American. Choose one of those examples and explain how it helps you as a reader to understand her feelings.

Writing Assignments

1. Sounds and silence are strong memories of Kingston's early years in school. Write an essay about a dominant sensory memory from

your first school experience. You might recall the smells from the cafeteria, the squeak of chalk on the blackboard, or the sight of the playground through the classroom window. Explain how these sensory images contributed to your sense of being somewhere other than home.

2. Kingston describes the actions of a number of teachers who appear to be ignorant of the reasons for her and her sister's behavior in school. How sensitive or knowledgeable about the different cultures of students should teachers be? Write an essay explaining what you think the responsibility of the school is in integrating non-native children into American culture.

I Think, Therefore IM

Jennifer Lee

Jennifer Lee (1976–) was born in New York City. She graduated from Harvard University in 1999 with a degree in mathematics and economics. While at Harvard she spent a year at Beijing University on a fellowship studying international relations. Lee has received a scholarship from the Asian American Journalism Association and has interned at The Boston Globe, The New York Times, Newsday, The Wall Street Journal, *and* The Washington Post. *She joined the staff of* The New York Times *in 2001 as a technology reporter and began writing for the Metro section the next year. The following selection on instant-messaging language originally appeared in the* Times *in September 2002.*

1 Each September Jacqueline Harding prepares a classroom presentation on the common writing mistakes she sees in her students' work. 1

Ms. Harding, an eighth-grade English teacher at Viking Middle School in Guernee, Ill., scribbles the words that have plagued generations of school children across her whiteboard:

There. Their. They're.
Your. You're.
To. Too. Two.
Its. It's.

This September, she has added a new list: u, r, ur, b4, wuz, cuz, 2.

When she asked her students how many of them used shortcuts like them in their writing, Ms. Harding said, she was not surprised when most of them raised their hands. This, after all, is their online lingua franca: English adapted for the spitfire conversational style of Internet instant messaging.

Ms. Harding, who has seen such shortcuts creep into student papers over the last two years, said she gave her students a warning: "If I see this in your assignments, I will take points off."

5 "Kids should know the difference," said Ms. Harding, who decided to address this issue head-on this year. "They should know where to draw the line between formal writing and conversational writing."

As more and more teenagers socialize online, middle school and high school teachers like Ms. Harding are increasingly seeing a breezy form of Internet English jump from e-mail into schoolwork. To their dismay, teachers say that papers are being written with shortened words, improper capitalization and punctuation, and characters like &, $ and @.

Teachers have deducted points, drawn red circles and tsk-tsked at their classes. Yet the errant forms continue. "It stops being funny after you repeat yourself a couple of times," Ms. Harding said.

But teenagers, whose social life can rely as much these days on text communication as the spoken word, say that they use instant-messaging shorthand without thinking about it. They write to one another as much as they write in school, or more.

"You are so used to abbreviating things, you just start doing it unconsciously on schoolwork and reports and other things," said Eve Brecker, 15, a student at Montclair High School in New Jersey.

10 Ms. Brecker once handed in a midterm exam riddled with instant-messaging shorthand. "I had an hour to write an essay on *Romeo and Juliet,*" she said. "I just wanted to finish before my time was up. I was writing fast and carelessly. I spelled 'you' 'u.'" She got a C.

Even terms that cannot be expressed verbally are making their way into papers. Melanie Weaver was stunned by some of the term papers she received from a 10th-grade class she recently taught as part of an internship. "They would be trying to make a point in a paper, they would put a smiley face in the end," said Ms. Weaver, who teaches at Alvernia College in Reading, PA. "If they were presenting an argument and they needed to present an opposite view, they would put a frown."

As Trisha Fogarty, a sixth-grade teacher at Houlton Southside School in Houlton, Maine, puts it, today's students are "Generation Text."

Almost 60 percent of the online population under age 17 uses instant messaging, according to Nielsen/NetRatings. In addition to cellphone text messaging, Weblogs and e-mail, it has become a popular means of flirting, setting up dates, asking for help with homework and keeping in contact with distant friends. The abbreviations are a natural outgrowth of this rapid-fire style of communication.

"They have a social life that centers around typed communication," said Judith S. Donath, a professor at the Massachusetts Institute of Technology's Media Lab who has studied electronic communication. "They have a writing style that has been nurtured in a teenage social milieu."

15 Some teachers see the creeping abbreviations as part of a continuing assault of technology on formal written English. Others take it more lightly, saying that it is just part of the larger arc of language evolution.

"To them it's not wrong," said Ms. Harding, who is 28. "It's acceptable because it's in their culture. It's hard enough to teach them the art of formal writing. Now we've got to overcome this new instant-messaging language."

Ms. Harding noted that in some cases the shorthand isn't even shorter. "I understand 'cuz,' but what's with the 'wuz'? It's the same amount of letters as 'was,' so what's the point?" she said.

Deborah Bova, who teaches eighth-grade English at Raymond Park Middle School in Indianapolis, thought her eyesight was failing several years ago when she saw the sentence "B4 we perform, ppl have 2 practice" on a student assignment.

"I thought, 'My God, what is this?' " Ms. Bova said. "Have they lost their minds?"

20 The student was summoned to the board to translate the sentence into standard English: "Before we perform, people have to practice." She realized that the students thought she was out of touch. "It was like 'Get with it, Bova,' " she said. Ms. Bova had a student type up a reference list of translations for common instant-messaging expressions. She posted a copy on the bulletin board by her desk and took another one home to use while grading.

Students are sometimes unrepentant.

"They were astonished when I began to point these things out to them," said Henry Assetto, a social studies teacher at Twin Valley High School in Elverson, Pa. "Because I am a history teacher, they did not think a history teacher would be checking up on their grammar or their spelling," said Mr. Assetto, who has been teaching for 34 years.

But Montana Hodgen, 16, another Montclair student, said she was so accustomed to instant-messaging abbreviations that she often read right past them. She proofread a paper last year only to get it returned with the messaging abbreviations circled in red.

"I was so used to reading what my friends wrote to me on Instant Messenger that I didn't even realize that there was something wrong," she said. She said her ability to separate formal and informal English declined the more she used instant messages. "Three years ago, if I had seen that, I would have been 'What is that?' "

25 The spelling checker doesn't always help either, students say. For one, Microsoft Word's squiggly red spell-check lines don't appear beneath single letters and numbers such as u, r, c, 2 and 4. Nor do they catch words which have numbers in them such as "l8r" and "b4" by default.

Teenagers have essentially developed an unconscious "accent" in their typing, Professor Donath said. "They have gotten facile at typing and they are not paying attention."

Teenagers have long pushed the boundaries of spoken language, introducing words that then become passe with adult adoption. Now teenagers are taking charge and pushing the boundaries of written language. For them, expressions like "oic" (oh I see), "nm" (not much), "jk" (just kidding) and "lol" (laughing out loud), "brb" (be right back), "ttyl" (talk to you later) are as standard as conventional English.

"There is no official English language," said Jesse Sheidlower, the North American editor of the *Oxford English Dictionary.* "Language is spread not because anyone dictates any one thing to happen. The decisions are made by the language and the people who use the language."

Some teachers find the new writing style alarming. "First of all, it's very rude, and it's very careless," said Lois Moran, a middle school English teacher at St. Nicholas School in Jersey City.

30 "They should be careful to write properly and not to put these little codes in that they are in such a habit of writing to each other," said Ms. Moran, who has lectured her eighth-grade class on such mistakes.

Others say that the instant-messaging style might simply be a fad, something that students will grow out of. Or they see it as an opportunity to teach students about the evolution of language.

"I turn it into a very positive teachable moment for kids in the class," said Erika V. Karres, an assistant professor at the University of North Carolina at Chapel Hill who trains student teachers. She shows students how English has evolved since Shakespeare's time. "Imagine Langston Hughes's writing in quick texting instead of 'Langston writing,' " she said. "It makes teaching and learning so exciting."

Other teachers encourage students to use messaging shorthand to spark their thinking processes. "When my children are writing first drafts, I don't care how they spell anything, as long as they are writing," said Ms. Fogarty, the sixth-grade teacher from Houlton, Maine. "If this lingo gets their thoughts and ideas onto paper quicker, the more power to them." But during editing and revising, she expects her students to switch to standard English.

Ms. Bova shares the view that instant-messaging language can help free up their creativity. With the help of students, she does not even need the cheat sheet to read the shorthand anymore.

"I think it's a plus," she said. "And I would say that with a + sign."

Questions on Meaning

1. What are the social and technological conditions that have shaped cyberlingo vocabulary and its uses?
2. What does the term "lingua franca" mean? How does it capture the full significance of the text messaging style of young people?
3. Why, in your opinion, are adults frequently appalled when students use an informal or unconventional style in their writing?

Questions on Rhetorical Strategy and Style

1. Why does Lee open her article with the words Ms. Harding puts on the board each September? What is she trying to suggest to her readers?
2. How does the article adhere to the conventions of the newspaper journalism? Does the writer remain balanced and objective? Explain how.
3. Why does the writer quote the editor of the *Oxford English Dictionary?*

Writing Assignments

1. Why do teachers often seem fussy, and even offended, by their students' use of language? Why are they so insistent about the conventions of standard, edited English? Write an essay that explains to your teachers your experience trying to learn these conventions, and why your language is necessary to your sense of identity.
2. Try the exercise used by Erika Karres, the teacher at the University of North Carolina. Take a poem or any piece of writing and translate it into a quick text version. How does the meaning of it change?

Essays on Life

Generation X

Kirsten Cole

Journalist Kirsten Cole wrote this article for The Observer *on the generation who followed the Baby Boomers. The label "Generation X" characterizes a group similar in some ways to the "Beat" generation, who preceded the Boomers. Like the Beats, Xers profess spiritual rootlessness and prefer a transient style of life and career. In particular they define their values against those of the Boomers, as the Beats defined their values against those of their parents, the generation reared during the Depression and the Second World War. Douglas Coupland's book,* Generation X: Tales for An Accelerated Culture *is the definitive source on this group's values. In the article reprinted here, Cole introduces the concept of Generation X through example and interview.*

1 Do you remember seeing *Star Wars* on the big screen? Was one of your favorite childhood games Atari? Did you spend your teenage years wanting your MTV? 1

A "yes" answer to one or more of those questions may mean you are one of 44 million people between the ages of 18 and 29 and a member of Generation X.

The generation following the baby boom is slowly creeping into the spotlight. As the boomers age, advertisers, marketers and media have begun to recognize and pay attention to this new group, which has been saddled with such titles as "baby busters," the "bland generation," "13ers," "twentysomethings," "slackers," the "repair generation," "post-boomers," "Xers," and the "shadow generation."

This generation represents a $125 billion market. But thanks to its one commonalty, diversity, everyone—including the media, advertisers and just about everybody else—are having a hard time defining Generation X.

Heidi Shields, 25, of Chicago, fits many media definitions of an Xer. She graduated from college in 1991 with a degree in graphic arts.

"When I started college, computer graphic people were in demand," she said. "When I got out of college, the market was completely saturated. There had been cutbacks in the field, so people with 20 years experience were back in the market. It made sense, but I thought, 'it's our turn.' "

So, like an estimated 58 percent of all unmarried singles age 20 to 24, Shields moved back home and began a two-year search for a job in her field.

Also, like many of her contemporaries, she took several jobs, none career-related, just to pay the bills and save a little money.

"I knew it was going to be hard, but I didn't think it would take two years," Shields said. "I searched endlessly for a job in the Peoria area (where she was from). I would have liked to stay in Peoria but I was scared to be too far out of school without any experience."

Shields ended up working four jobs, including bartending and painting sweatshirts with her sister, to save up enough money to move to Chicago.

Shields was able to find a job in computer graphics in Chicago. Although she doesn't plan on staying with the company for a long time, she sees it as a stepping stone.

"I want something more challenging. This job is not very creative," Shields said, "but I am definitely getting experience. Ultimately, I would like to do freelance graphics for people."

"I may be living check to check right now, but I am not at the total bottom. I am trying to stay optimistic for sure."

Shields falls in the middle of the generation, whereas Tom Sargeant, 28, accountant supervisor for Resource Marketing, which is a division of R & B Productions, falls at the tail end.

Sargeant, who found work almost immediately out of college, had a different outlook on employment than Shields. Although he didn't know for sure if the money he was spending on college would be worth it, he was banking on it.

"I figured it would ultimately pay off. I looked at college as an investment." he said. "My expectations haven't changed that drastically after college. I maintain the attitude the harder you work, the more money you make."

Some people claim baby busters are cynical about boomers. According to an article in *U.S. News and World Report* (Feb. 22, 1993), busters see boomers as "insufferably self-righteous yuppies who sold out their principles, placed work over family and money over community."

Sargeant, however, said there shouldn't be an "us against them philosophy."

"All we've talked about is baby boomers, so many people, so many years," he said. "Now, another generation wants the spotlight."

Twenty-four-year-old Eric Blankenburg agreed with Sargeant that baby boomers are not all to blame.

"Things were not perfect when they were born," he said. "It has progressively gone down hill and unfortunately things will get worse."

"Baby boomers say we are rebels or hooligans. I think we are exactly the opposite. Like people my age, 99 percent vote and honestly care about the future. Society needs to look at us as the future," he added. "They should work with us instead of against us."

Ellen Clore, 24, is not so convinced by people her age.

"Some are and some aren't more aware and active," she said. "I think the majority are apathetic, with a few that are very concerned. They don't watch the news or read the paper."

"Aspirations were not as high for the baby boomers. We (busters) have greater expectations, but they are harder to reach because it is more competitive," she added. "Back then, a high school diploma was equivalent to our college degree. Now we need to attend graduate school to get a good job."

Blankenburg, like Shields, discovered a degree doesn't automatically guarantee someone a job.

"I wanted the best job out of college. I thought after I graduated I could have any job I wanted and be making $35,000 a year." he said. "A week before graduation I said 'great a degree, the key to the world.' After graduation, reality hit me. It's not like that (receiving the dream job) and it still is not two years later."

Blankenburg, who works for Multi-Ad, did end up moving back home with his parents for several months. However, he did find work before they enforced a rent rule. Things have improved, but he is still a ways from the income level of his dreams.

He said he is living a lot check to check, even though living expenses are lower, due to a roommate. However, he blames this on the attitude, "the more you have, the more you spend."

"Among friends my age, it's typical to live like this. They are not doctors and lawyers," he said. "It is harder to make money for our generation."

"I know, our parents worked hard and climbed the ladder to be successful. It is time for us to take out ladders and start climbing. It may be longer, but we need to climb it just the same."

Clore, who is currently working at the Peoria Civic Center as a temporary executive assistant, was another Xer who discovered ways of cutting expenses, including living with her parents.

"I used to have a roommate and we split most everything," she said. "I didn't have car payments, so I had lower expenses. I worked in the suburbs of Chicago and took the train to work, which was cheaper."

Clore, who attended graduate school, also experienced a reality check after graduation.

"I really did believe the money spent on college would be worth it." she said. "I went to a private school, spent a lot of money and now have a lot of debt. I didn't make nearly as much money as I thought I would, but I will probably step up the ladder with my extra education."

Observing the struggle of peers has created somewhat of a pessimistic attitude at the lower end of Xers. Steve Szymke, 18, expects there is going to be a struggle after graduating from Bradley University.

"I see my friends that don't have jobs," said Szymke, who dreams of directing films one day. "In the movie industry, it's a real struggle to get above water. But, I have a definite advantage over those who don't have a degree. A person also needs the extra edge of graduate school."

"I am sure there will be a rude awakening for a lot of us, but now we sit around at Lums and think we know everything. We pretend we are solving the world's problems."

Contrary to Clore's concern about the involvement of Xers, Szymke votes and also reads, not fluffy material, but *Time.* He does agree that attitudes have changed.

"In the '60s kids cared about political things. Now, kids are into activism and have stances on abortion, environmental issues and religion," he said. "Our political involvement is nowhere near the '60s involvement."

Szymke is also aware that money isn't a bumper crop.

"My first semester of college I would spend a dollar here and another one there," he said. "I figured out quickly that it adds up. And although my dad is helping quite a bit with college, I still have to pay for my graduate work."

Reportedly, three quarters of college professors say students are very unprepared in basic skills. Szymke, a sophomore at Bradley University, doesn't dispute that fact.

"I was lucky when I went to Dunlap, but there were some students from California at Bradley who studied in public schools," he said. "They are really bad and don't know how to study. They also don't know how to take tests."

Though there are common links in attitude, like the group's bleak economic and financial future, the common denominator for the group, as Sargeant said, is diversity. That may explain the term "Generation X."

"There is no given for "X." It's a variable. It's not an acronym," he said. "You can't put the same values in place of the variable for everyone.

"I think we are lost," Szymke said. "There are so many variables and things are so uncertain. Maybe X means exploration."

"I think we associate with material things rather than an economic situation. We were asked to categorize Generation X in an art class. They asked people if they remembered seeing *Star Wars* on the big screen," he added. "If you said yes, they said, 'Well, then you're a member of Generation X.' Look at MTV, too, it's the channel for 18–27 year olds."

And if Generation X is recognized as the Atari and MTV generation, then what's in store for the next generation?

"We'll probably have the Nintendo generation next." Szymke said, laughing.

Key Terms

Atari
saturated
contemporaries
bumper crop
denominator
acronym
variable

Questions on Meaning

1. How does Cole define Generation X? List the traits she mentions. With how many of these do you identify?
2. According to the article from *U.S. News and World Report* cited in Cole's essay, why are members of Generation X cynical about baby boomers?
3. Of the Generation Xers Cole writes about, which one appeals to you most? Why?

Questions on Rhetorical Strategy and Style

1. Why does Cole profile these particular five people in her article? What does she want to have us to believe?
2. What is Cole's main point? Where in the article is it revealed?
3. How much interview material has Cole used in her article? What purpose does the quoted material serve?

Writing Assignments

1. This article was published in 1993 and related to people who were 18 to 29 at that time. What generation do you consider yourself a member of now? Write an essay in which you compare this generation of 18- to 29-year-old people with those in that age group from the early 1990s. Discuss the similar and differing values, experience, and lifestyle.
2. Write a profile of someone you know from Generation X. What is this person up to now? How has he or she changed?

We Talk, You Listen

Vine Deloria, Jr.

Vine Deloria (1933–) was born in South Dakota and reared in the Standing Rock Sioux Reservation community. He graduated from Iowa State University (B. S.) and Rock Island Lutheran School (M. S. in theology), and received a law degree from the University of Colorado. A well-known Native American activist, Deloria has served as executive director of the National Congress of American Indians (1964–1967) and chair of the Native American Studies program at the University of Arizona. Deloria's books include Custer Died for Your Sins: An Indian Manifesto *(1969),* God is Red: A Native View of Religion *(1973),* We Talk, You Listen: New Tribes, New Turf *(1970), and* Behind the Trail of Broken Treaties: An Indian Declaration of Independence *(1974). In this 1970 essay from* We Talk, You Listen, *Deloria describes how both media stereotypes and college ethnic studies programs affect the self-image of the members of minority groups.*

1 One reason that Indian people have not been heard from until 1
recently is that we have been completely covered up by movie Indians. Western movies have been such favorites that they have dominated the public's conception of what Indians are. It is not all bad when one thinks about the handsome Jay Silverheels bailing the Lone Ranger out of a jam, or Ed Ames rescuing Daniel Boone with some clever Indian trick. But the other mythologies that have wafted skyward because of the movies have blocked out any idea that there might be real Indians with real problems.

Other minority groups have fought tenaciously against stereotyping, and generally they have been successful. Italians quickly quashed the image of them as mobsters that television projected in *The Untouchables.* Blacks have been successful in getting a more realistic picture of the black man in a contemporary setting because they have had standout performers like Bill Cosby and Sidney Poitier to represent them.

Since stereotyping was highlighted by motion pictures, it would probably be well to review the images of minority groups projected in the movies in order to understand how the situation looks at present. Perhaps the first aspect of stereotyping was the tendency to exclude people on the basis of their inability to handle the English language. Not only were racial minorities excluded, but immigrants arriving on these shores were soon whipped into shape by ridicule of their English.

Traditional stereotypes pictured the black as a happy watermelon-eating darky whose sole contribution to American society was his indiscriminate substitution of the "d" sound for "th." Thus a black always said "dis" and "dat," as in "lift dat bale." The "d" sound carried over and was used by white gangsters to indicate disfavor with their situation, as in "dis is de end, ya rat." The important thing was to indicate that blacks were like lisping children not yet competent to undertake the rigors of economic opportunities and voting.

Mexicans were generally portrayed as shiftless and padded out for siesta, without any redeeming qualities whatsoever. Where the black had been handicapped by his use of the "d," the Mexican suffered from the use of the double "e." This marked them off as a group worth watching. Mexicans, according to the stereotype, always said "theenk," "peenk," and later "feenk." Many advertisements today still continue this stereotype, thinking that it is cute and cuddly.

These groups were much better off than Indians were. Indians were always devoid of any English whatsoever. They were only allowed to speak when an important message had to be transmitted on the screen. For example, "many pony soldiers die" was meant to indicate that Indians were going to attack the peaceful settlers who happened to have broken their three hundredth treaty moments before. Other than that Indian linguistic ability was limited to "ugh" and "kemo sabe" (which means honky in some obscure Indian language).

The next step was to acknowledge that there was a great American dream to which any child could aspire. (It was almost like the train in the night that Richard Nixon heard as a child anticipating the dream fairy.) The great American dream was projected in the early World War II movies. The last reel was devoted to a stirring proclamation that we were going to win the war and it showed factories producing airplanes, people building ships, and men marching in uniform to the transports. There was a quick pan of a black face before the scene shifted to scenes of orchards, rivers, Mount Rushmore, and the Liberty Bell as we found out what we were fighting for.

The new images expressed a profound inability to understand why minority groups couldn't "make it" when everybody knew what America was all about freedom and equality. By projecting an image of everyone working hard to win the war, the doctrine was spread that America was just one big happy family and that there really weren't any differences so long as we had to win the war.

It was a rare war movie in the 1940s that actually showed a black or a Mexican as a bona fide fighting man. When they did appear it was in the role of cooks or orderlies serving whites. In most cases this was a fairly accurate statement of their situation, particularly with respect to the Navy.

World War II movies were entirely different for Indians. Each platoon of red-blooded white American boys was equipped with its own set of Indians. When the platoon got into trouble and was surrounded, its communications cut off except for one slender line to regimental headquarters, and that line tapped by myriads of Germans, Japanese, or Italians, the stage was set for the dramatic episode of the Indians.

John Wayne, Randolph Scott, Sonny Tufts, or Tyrone Power would smile broadly as he played his ace, which until this time had been hidden from view. From nowhere, a Navaho, Comanche, Cherokee, or Sioux would appear, take the telephone, and in some short and inscrutable phraseology communicate such a plenitude of knowledge to his fellow tribesman (fortunately situated at the general's right hand) that fighting units thousands of miles away would instantly perceive the situation and rescue the platoon. The Indian would disappear as mysteriously as he had come, only to reappear the next week in a different battle to perform his esoteric rites. Anyone watching war movies during the '40s would have been convinced that without Indian telephone operators the war would have been lost irretrievably, in spite of John Wayne.

Indians were America's secret weapon against the forces of evil. The typing spoke of a primitive gimmick, and it was the strangeness of Indians that made them visible, not their humanity. With the Korean War era and movies made during the middle '50s, other minority groups began to appear and Indians were pushed into the background. This era was the heyday of the "All-American Platoon." It was the ultimate conception of intergroup relations. The "All-American Platoon" was a "one each": one black, one Mexican, one Indian, one farm boy from Iowa, one Southerner who hated blacks, one boy from Brooklyn, one Polish boy from the urban slums of the Midwest, one Jewish intellectual, and one college boy. Every possible stereotype was included and it resulted in a portrayal of Indians as another species of human being for the first time in moving pictures.

The platoon was always commanded by a veteran of grizzled countenance who had been at every battle in which the United States had ever engaged. The whole story consisted in killing off the members of the platoon until only the veteran and the college boy were left. The Southerner and the black would die in each other's arms singing "Dixie." The Jewish intellectual and the Indian formed some kind of attachment and were curiously the last ones killed. When the smoke cleared, the college boy, with a prestige wound in the shoulder, returned to his girl, and the veteran reconciled with his wife and checked out another platoon in anticipation of taking the same hill in the next movie.

While other groups have managed to make great strides since those days, Indians have remained the primitive unknown quantity. Dialogue has reverted back to the monosyllabic grunt and even pictures that attempt to present the Indian side of the story depend upon unintelligible noises to present their message. The only exception to this rule is a line famed for its durability over the years. If you fall asleep during the Late Show and suddenly awaken to the words "go in peace, my son," it is either an Indian chief bidding his son good bye as the boy heads for college or a Roman Catholic priest forgiving Paul Newman or Steve McQueen for killing a hundred men in the preceding reel.

15 Anyone raising questions about the image of minority groups as portrayed in television and the movies is automatically suspect as an un-American and subversive influence on the minds of the young. The historical, linguistic, and cultural differences are neatly blocked out by the fad of portraying members of minority groups in roles which formerly were reserved for whites. Thus Burt Reynolds played

a Mohawk detective busy solving the crime problem in New York City. Diahann Carroll played a well-to-do black widow with small child in a television series that was obviously patterned after the unique single-headed white family.

In recent years the documentary has arisen to present the story of Indian people and a number of series on Black America have been produced. Indian documentaries are singularly the same. A reporter and television crew hasten to either the Navaho or Pine Ridge reservation, quickly shoot reels on poverty conditions, and return East blithely thinking that they have captured the essence of Indian life. In spite of the best intentions, the eternal yearning to present an exciting story of a strange people overcomes, and the endless cycle of poverty-oriented films continues.

This type of approach continually categorizes the Indian as an incompetent boob who can't seem to get along and who is hopelessly mired in a poverty of his own making. Hidden beneath these documentaries is the message that Indians really want to live this way. No one has yet filmed the incredible progress that is being made by the Makah tribe, the Quinaults, Red Lake Chippewas, Gila River Pima-Maricopas, and others. Documentaries project the feeling that reservations should be eliminated because the conditions are so bad. There is no effort to present the bright side of Indian life.

With the rise of ethnic studies programs and courses in minority group history, the situation has become worse. People who support these programs assume that by communicating the best aspects of a group they have somehow solved the major problems of that group in its relations with the rest of society. By emphasizing that black is beautiful or that Indians have contributed the names of rivers to the road map, many people feel that they have done justice to the group concerned.

One theory of interpretation of Indian history that has arisen in the past several years is that all of the Indian war chiefs were patriots defending their lands. This is the "patriot chief" interpretation of history. Fundamentally it is a good theory in that it places a more equal balance to interpreting certain Indian wars as wars of resistance. It gets away from the tendency, seen earlier in this century, to classify all Indian warriors as renegades. But there is a tendency to overlook the obvious renegades—Indians who were treacherous and would have been renegades had there been no whites to fight. The patriot chiefs interpretation also conveniently overlooks the fact that every significant leader of the previous century was eventually done in by his own people in one way or another. Sitting Bull was killed by Indian police working for the government. Geronimo was captured by an army led by Apache scouts who sided with the United States.

If the weak points of each minority group's history are to be covered over by a sweetness-and-light interpretation based on what we would like to think happened rather than what did happen, we doom ourselves to decades of further racial strife. Most of the study programs today emphasize the goodness that is inherent in the different minority communities, instead of trying to present a balanced story. There are basically two schools of interpretation running through all of these efforts as the demand for black, red, and brown pride dominates the programs.

One theory derives from the "All-American Platoon" concept of a decade ago. Under this theory members of the respective racial minority groups had an important role in the great events of American history. Crispus Attucks, a black, almost single-handedly started the Revolutionary War, while Eli Parker, the Seneca Indian general, won the Civil War and would have concluded it sooner had not there been so many stupid whites abroad in those days. This is the "cameo" theory of history. It takes a basic "manifest destiny" white interpretation of history and lovingly plugs a few feathers, woolly heads, and sombreros into the famous events of American history. No one tries to explain what an Indian is who was helping the whites destroy his own people, since we are now all Americans and have these great events in common.

The absurdity of the cameo school of ethnic pride is self-apparent. Little Mexican children are taught that there were some good Mexicans at the Alamo. They can therefore be happy that Mexicans have been involved in the significant events of Texas history. Little is said about the Mexicans on the other side at the Alamo. The result is a denial of a substantial Mexican heritage by creating the feeling that "we all did it together." If this trend continues I would not be surprised to discover that Columbus had a Cherokee on board when he set sail from Spain in search of the Indies.

The cameo school smothers any differences that existed historically by presenting a history in which all groups have participated through representatives. Regardless of Crispus Attucks's valiant behavior during the Revolution, it is doubtful that he envisioned another century of slavery for blacks as a cause worth defending.

The other basic school of interpretation is a projection backward of the material blessings of the white middle class. It seeks to identify where all the material wealth originated and finds that each minority group *contributed* something. It can therefore be called the contribution school. Under this conception we should all love Indians because they contributed corn, squash, potatoes, tobacco, coffee, rubber, and other agricultural products. In like manner, blacks and Mexicans are credited with Carver's work on the peanut, blood transfusion, and tacos and tamales.

The ludicrous implication of the contribution school visualizes the minority groups clamoring to enter American society, lined up with an abundance of foods and fancies, presenting them to whites in a never ending stream of generosity. If the different minority groups were given an overriding two-percent royalty on their contributions, the same way whites have managed to give themselves royalties for their inventions, this school would have a more realistic impact on minority groups.

The danger with both of these types of ethnic studies theories is that they present an unrealistic account of the role of minority groups in American history. Certainly there is more to the story of the American Indian than providing cocoa and popcorn for Columbus's landing party. When the clashes of history are smoothed over in favor of a mushy togetherness feeling, then people begin to wonder what has happened in the recent past that has created the conditions of today. It has been the feeling of younger people that contemporary problems have arisen because community leadership has been consistently betraying them. Older statesmen are called Uncle Toms, and the entire fabric of accumulated wisdom and experience of the older generation of minority groups is destroyed. . . .

Under present conceptions of ethnic studies there can be no lasting benefit either to minority groups or to society at large. The pride that can be built into children and youth by acknowledgment of the validity of their group certainly cannot be built by simply transferring symbols and interpretations arising in white culture history into an Indian, black, or Mexican setting. The result will be to make the minority groups bear the white man's burden by using his symbols and stereotypes as if they were their own.

There must be a drive within each minority group to understand its own uniqueness. This can only be done by examining what experiences were relevant to the group, not what experiences of white America the group wishes itself to be represented in. As an example, the discovery of gold in California was a significant event in the experience of white America. The discovery itself was irrelevant to the western Indian tribes, but the migrations caused by the discovery of gold were vitally important. The two histories can dovetail around this topic but ultimately each interpretation must depend upon its orientation to the group involved.

What has been important and continues to be important is the Constitution of the United States and its continual adaptation to contemporary situations. With the Constitution as a framework and reference point, it would appear that a number of conflicting interpretations of the experience of America could be validly given. While they might conflict at every point as each group defines to its own satisfaction what its experience has meant, recognition that within the Constitutional framework we are engaged in a living process of intergroup relationships would mean that no one group could define the meaning of American society to the exclusion of any other.

Self-awareness of each group must define a series of histories about the American experience. Manifest destiny has dominated thinking in the past because it has had an abstract quality that appeared to interpret experiences accurately. Nearly every racial and ethnic group has had to bow down before this conception of history and conform to an understanding of the world that it did not ultimately believe. Martin Luther King, Jr., spoke to his people on the basis of self-awareness the night before he died. He told them that they as a people would reach the promised land. Without the same sense of destiny, minority groups will simply be adopting the outmoded forms of stereotyping by which whites have deluded themselves for centuries.

We can survive as a society if we reject the conquest-oriented interpretation of the Constitution. While some Indian nationalists want the whole country back, a guarantee of adequate protection of existing treaty rights would provide a meaningful compromise. The Constitution should provide a sense of balance between groups as it has between conflicting desires of individuals.

As each group defines the ideas and doctrines necessary to maintain its own sense of dignity and identity, similarities in goals can be drawn that will have relevance beyond immediate group aspirations. Stereotyping will change radically because the ideological basis for portraying the members of any group will depend on that group's values. Plots in books and movies will have to show life as it is seen from within the group. Society will become broader and more cosmopolitan as innovative themes are presented to it. The universal sense of inhumanity will take on an aspect of concreteness. From the variety of cultural behavior patterns we can devise a new understanding of humanity.

The problem of stereotyping is not so much a racial problem as it is problem of limited knowledge and perspective. Even though minority groups have suffered in the past by ridiculous characterizations of themselves by white society, they must not fall into the same trap by simply reversing the process that has stereotyped them. Minority groups must thrust through the rhetorical blockade by creating within themselves a sense of "peoplehood." This ultimately means the creation of a new history and not mere amendments to the historical interpretations of white America.

Questions on Meaning

1. What is Deloria's thesis? What examples does he include to support this view?
2. In his discussion of the "theories of interpretation" employed by ethnic study programs, what does Deloria mean by the "cameo" and "projection backward" schools of ethnic pride? What are the dangers with these interpretations of history that he cites?
3. Describe the "new history" of white America that Deloria advocates.

Questions on Rhetorical Strategy and Style

1. How does Deloria compare and contrast the early movie stereotyping of Indians, Mexicans, and African-Americans with regard to language, the "great American dream," and wartime? How have the movie images of these three ethnic groups changed since the early days of film? Why do you think he does not include the Asian-American or the broader Hispanic-American ethnic groups in this discussion?
2. Analyze the process that Deloria says each minority group must use to "understand its own uniqueness." What is the role of the U.S. Constitution?
3. Examine how Deloria uses causation to explain the negative impact of documentaries on Indians. What does he suggest that would help present correct images of Indians?

Writing Assignments

1. Compare and contrast the portrayals of Indians, Asians, blacks, and Hispanics you have seen recently on television or in the movies to your own perceptions of these ethnic groups. What are the stereotypes? How have the media images changed since Deloria wrote this essay?
2. Choose one of the ethnic heroes of American history mentioned by Deloria—Crispus Attucks or Eli Parker—and learn about their life and their role in American history. In particular, find children's books that provide short, simple biographies of these men. Is the person you chose given a cameo appearance in history, as Deloria charges, or is his role given in a proper perspective?

3. Read the Constitution of the United States, including the Preamble and its Amendments. Do you believe the Constitution can "provide a balance between groups" as Deloria suggests? Write an essay on the role the Constitution should play in providing a "sense of dignity and identity" to the various ethnic groups that comprise America. Do you agree with Deloria that the Constitution does not permit one group to "define the meaning of America" to the exclusion of others?

On Self-Respect

Joan Didion

Joan Didion (1934–) was born in Sacramento, California. She received a B.A. at the University of California at Berkeley in 1956, then moved to New York City, where she spent seven years working as an associate editor at Vogue *and as a contributor to* Esquire, *the* National Review, *and the* Saturday Evening Post. *In 1964, Didion married writer John Gregory Dunne and went back to California, where she began to write the essays and fiction that became her genre: personal commentaries on contemporary events that expose social disintegration. Her published works include the collections of essays* Slouching Towards Bethlehem *(1968),* The White Album *(1970), and* After Henry *(1992); the novels* Run River *(1963),* Play It As It Lays *(1970),* A Book of Common Prayer *(1977), and* Democracy *(1984); and the nonfiction books* Salvador *(1983),* Miami *(1987),* Political Fictions *(2001),* Where I Was From *(2003), and* The Year of Magical Thinking *(2005), for which she won the National Book Award for nonfiction. Didion looks inward in this essay, leveling her sometimes terse, always sharp commentary on herself and on the rest of us.*

1 Once, in a dry season, I wrote in large letters across two pages 1
of a notebook that innocence ends when one is stripped of the delusion that one likes oneself. Although now, some years later, I marvel that a mind on the outs with itself should have nonetheless made painstaking record of its every tremor, I recall with embarrassing clarity the flavor of those particular ashes. It was a matter of misplaced self-respect.

I had not been elected to Phi Beta Kappa. This failure could scarcely have been more predictable or less ambiguous (I simply did not have the grades), but I was unnerved by it; I had somehow thought myself a kind of academic Raskolnikov, curiously exempt from the cause-effect relationships which hampered others. Although even the humorless nineteen-year-old that I was must have recognized that the situation lacked real tragic stature, the day that I did not make Phi Beta Kappa nonetheless marked the end of something, and innocence may well be the word for it. I lost the conviction that lights would always turn green for me, the pleasant certainty that those rather passive virtues which had won me approval as a child automatically guaranteed me not only Phi Beta Kappa keys but happiness, honor, and the love of a good man; lost a certain touching faith in the totem power of good manners, clean hair, and proven competence on the Stanford-Binet scale. To such doubtful amulets had my self-respect been pinned, and I faced myself that day with the nonplused apprehension of someone who has come across a vampire and has no crucifix at hand.

Although to be driven back upon oneself is an uneasy affair at best, rather like trying to cross a border with borrowed credentials, it seems to me now the one condition necessary to the beginnings of real self-respect. Most of our platitudes notwithstanding, self-deception remains the most difficult deception. The tricks that work on others count for nothing in that very well-lit back alley where one keeps assignations with oneself: no winning smiles will do here, no prettily drawn lists of good intentions. One shuffles flashily but in vain through one's marked cards—the kindness done for the wrong reason, the apparent triumph which involved no real effort, the seemingly heroic act into which one had been shamed. The dismal fact is that self-respect has nothing to do with the approval of others—who are, after all, deceived easily enough; has nothing to do with reputation, which, as Rhett Butler told Scarlett O'Hara, is something people with courage can do without.

To do without self-respect, on the other hand, is to be an unwilling audience of one to an interminable documentary that details one's failings, both real and imagined, with fresh footage spliced in for every screening. *There's the glass you broke in anger, there's the hurt on X's face; watch now, this next scene, the night Y came back from Houston, see how you muff this one.* To live without self-respect is to lie awake some night, beyond the reach of warm milk, phenobarbital, and the sleeping hand on the coverlet, counting up the sins of commission and omission, the trusts betrayed, the promises subtly broken, the gifts irrevocably wasted through sloth or cowardice or carelessness. However long we postpone it, we eventually lie down alone in that notoriously uncomfortable bed, the one we make ourselves. Whether or not we sleep in it depends, of course, on whether or not we respect ourselves.

5 To protest that some fairly improbable people, some people who *could not possibly respect themselves,* seem to sleep easily enough is to miss the point entirely, as surely as those people miss it who think that self-respect has necessarily to do with not having safety pins in one's underwear. There is a common superstition that "self-respect" is a kind of charm against snakes, something that keeps those who have it locked in some unblighted Eden, out of strange beds, ambivalent conversations, and trouble in general. It does not at all. It has nothing to do with the face of things, but concerns instead a separate peace, a private reconciliation. Although the careless, suicidal Julian English in *Appointment in Samarra* and the careless, incurably dishonest Jordan Baker in *The Great Gatsby* seem equally improbable candidates for self-respect, Jordan Baker had it, Julian English did not. With that genius for accommodation more often seen in women than in men, Jordan took her own measure, made her own peace, avoided threats to that peace: "I hate careless people," she told Nick Carraway. "It takes two to make an accident."

Like Jordan Baker, people with self-respect have the courage of their mistakes. They know the price of things. If they choose to commit adultery, they do not then go running, in an excess of bad conscience, to receive absolution from the wronged parties; nor do they complain unduly of the unfairness, the undeserved embarrassment, of being named correspondent. In brief, people with self-respect exhibit a certain toughness, a kind of moral nerve; they display what was once called *character,* a quality which, although approved in the abstract, sometimes loses ground to other, more instantly negotiable virtues. The measure of its slipping prestige is that one tends to think of it only in connection with homely children and United States senators who have been defeated, preferably in the primary, for reelection. Nonetheless, character—the willingness to accept responsibility for one's own life—is the source from which self-respect springs.

Self-respect is something that our grandparents, whether or not they had it, knew all about. They had instilled in them, young, a certain discipline, the sense that one lives by doing things one does not particularly want to do, by putting fears and doubts to one side, by weighing immediate comforts against the ability of larger, even intangible, comforts. It seemed to the nineteenth century admirable, but not remarkable, that Chinese Gordon put on a clean white suit and held Khartoum against the Mahdi; it did not seem unjust that the way to free land in California involved death and difficulty and dirt. In a diary kept during the winter of 1846, an emigrating twelve-year-old named Narcissa Cornwall noted coolly: "Father was busy reading and did not notice that the house was being filled with strange Indians until Mother spoke about it." Even lacking any clue as to what Mother said, one can scarcely fail to be impressed by the entire incident: the father reading, the Indians filing in, the mother choosing the words that would not alarm, the child duly recording the event and noting further that those particular Indians were not, "fortunately for us," hostile. Indians were simply part of the *donnée.*

In one guise or another, Indians always are. Again, it is a question of recognizing that anything worth having has its price. People who respect themselves are willing to accept the risk that the Indians will be hostile, that the venture will go bankrupt, that the liaison may not turn out to be one in which *every day is a holiday because you're married to me.* They are willing to invest something of themselves; they may not play at all, but when they do play, they know the odds.

That kind of self-respect is a discipline, a habit of mind that can never be faked but can be developed, trained, coaxed forth. It was once suggested to me that, as an antidote to crying, I put my head in a paper bag. As it happens, there is a sound physiological reason, something to do with oxygen, for doing exactly that, but the psychological effect alone is incalculable: it is difficult in the extreme to continue fancying oneself Cathy in *Wuthering Heights* with one's head in a Food Fair bag. There is a similar case for all the small disciplines, unimportant in themselves; imagine maintaining any kind of swoon, commiserative or carnal, in a cold shower.

10 But those small disciplines are available only insofar as they represent larger ones. To say that Waterloo was won on the playing fields of Eton is not to say that Napoleon might have been saved by a crash program in cricket; to give formal dinners in the rain forest would be

pointless did not the candlelight flickering on the liana call forth deeper, stronger disciplines, values instilled long before. It is a kind of ritual, helping us to remember who and what we are. In order to remember it, one must have known it.

To have that sense of one's intrinsic worth which constitutes self-respect is potentially to have everything: the ability to discriminate, to love and to remain indifferent. To lack it is to be locked within oneself, paradoxically incapable of either love or indifference. If we do not respect ourselves, we are on the one hand forced to despise those who have so few resources as to consort with us, so little perception as to remain blind to our fatal weaknesses. On the other, we are peculiarly in thrall to everyone we see, curiously determined to live out—since our self-image is untenable—their false notions of us. We flatter ourselves by thinking this compulsion to please others an attractive trait: a gist for imaginative empathy, evidence of our willingness to give. Of *course* I will play Francesca to your Paolo, Helen Keller to anyone's Annie Sullivan: no expectation is too misplaced, no role too ludicrous. At the mercy of those we cannot but hold in contempt, we play roles doomed to failure before they are begun, each defeat generating fresh despair at the urgency of divining and meeting the next demand made upon us.

It is the phenomenon sometimes called "alienation from self." In its advanced stages, we no longer answer the telephone, because someone might want something; that we could say *no* without drowning in self-reproach is an idea alien to this game. Every encounter demands too much, tears the nerves, drains the will, and the specter of something as small as an unanswered letter arouses such disproportionate guilt that answering it becomes out of the question. To assign unanswered letters their proper weight, to free us from the expectations of others, to give us back to ourselves—there lies the great, the singular power of self-respect. Without it, one eventually discovers the final turn of the screw: one runs away to find oneself, and finds no one at home.

Questions on Meaning

1. Didion describes quite starkly the many facets of self-respect—what it is, how it is manifested, and why some have it and some seem not to. How important *is* self-respect to her? Present evidence from the essay.
2. Didion contends that self-respect "has nothing to do with the approval of others." She points out that although one person may lack respect for another person, the other person may possess great self-respect. Why? Do you agree?
3. What does Didion mean when she states that people with self-respect have the "courage of their mistakes"? Can you name some public figures in the United States who exhibit that trait?

Questions on Rhetorical Strategy and Style

1. This essay uses definition as its main rhetorical strategy. In addition to defining self-respect, however, Didion explores the meaning of a number of other terms. Identify two other terms she identifies and discuss how she uses them to support her definition of self-respect.
2. How does Didion also use a cause and effect strategy in this essay? Would you have written these passages differently if you had written the essay?

Writing Assignments

1. Write an essay about an incident in which your self-respect came into question. What prompted the incident? How did you handle it? What did you learn from it? Over the long run, how has it affected your self-respect? Consider such questions as you define your concept of self-respect.
2. Write an essay about another "self" characteristic—self-esteem. As Didion did in this essay, explore what self-esteem means, how self-esteem is exhibited, and, importantly, the influence one has over one's own self-esteem.

Landscape and Narrative

Barry Lopez

Barry Lopez (1945–) was born in New York and grew up in New York City and rural California. He attended the University of Notre Dame and the University of Oregon. Interested in nature and folklore, Lopez has traveled throughout much of the United States and to Australia, the Arctic, Africa, and Antarctica. He has written many books about nature and the environment, including Desert Notes *(1976),* Of Wolves and Men *(1978),* River Notes *(1979),* Winter Count *(1981),* Arctic Dreams *(1986), which won the National Book Award,* The Rediscovery of North America *(1991), and* Field Notes *(1994). The following essay was published in* Crossing Open Ground *(1989). Lopez has been widely praised for the way he examines both the surfaces and the subsurfaces of our natural world.*

1 One summer evening in a remote village in the Brooks Range 1
of Alaska, I sat among a group of men listening to hunting stories about the trapping and pursuit of animals. I was particularly interested in several incidents involving wolverine, in part because a friend of mine was studying wolverine in Canada, among the Cree, but, too, because I find this animal such an intense creature. To hear about its life is to learn more about fierceness.

Wolverines are not intentionally secretive, hiding their lives from view, but they are seldom observed. The range of their known behavior is less than that of, say, bears or wolves. Still, that evening no gratuitous details were set out. This was somewhat odd, for wolverine

---

From *Crossing Open Ground* (New York: Charles Scribner's Sons, 1988), originally appeared in *Harper's* (December 1984) under a different title. Copyright © 1984, 1988 by Barry Holstun Lopez.

easily excite the imagination; they can loom suddenly in the landscape with authority, with an aura larger than their compact physical dimensions, drawing one's immediate and complete attention. Wolverine also have a deserved reputation for resoluteness in the worst winters, for ferocious strength. But neither did these attributes induce the men to embellish.

I listened carefully to these stories, taking pleasure in the sharply observed detail surrounding the dramatic thread of events. The story I remember most vividly was about a man hunting a wolverine from a snow machine in the spring. He followed the animal's tracks for several miles over rolling tundra in a certain valley. Soon he caught sight ahead of a dark spot on the crest of a hill—the wolverine pausing to look back. The hunter was catching up, but each time he came over a rise the wolverine was looking back from the next rise, just out of range. The hunter topped one more rise and met the wolverine bounding toward him. Before he could pull his rifle from its scabbard the wolverine flew across the engine cowl and the windshield, hitting him square in the chest. The hunter scrambled his arms wildly, trying to get the wolverine out of his lap, and fell over as he did so. The wolverine jumped clear as the snow machine rolled over, and fixed the man with a stare. He had not bitten, not even scratched the man. Then the wolverine walked away. The man thought of reaching for the gun, but no, he did not.

The other stories were like this, not so much making a point as evoking something about contact with wild animals that would never be completely understood.

5 When the stories were over, four or five of us walked out of the home of our host. The surrounding land, in the persistent light of a far northern summer, was still visible for miles—the striated, pitched massifs of the Brooks Range; the shy, willow-lined banks of the John River flowing south from Anaktuvuk Pass; and the flat tundra plain, opening with great affirmation to the north. The landscape seemed alive because of the stories. It was precisely these ocherous tones, this kind of willow, exactly this austerity that had informed the wolverine narratives. I felt exhilaration, and a deeper confirmation of the stories. The mundane tasks which awaited me I anticipated now with pleasure. The stories had renewed in me a sense of the purpose of my life.

This feeling, an inexplicable renewal of enthusiasm after storytelling, is familiar to many people. It does not seem to matter greatly what the subject is, as long as the context is intimate and the story is told for its own sake, not forced to serve merely as the vehicle for an idea. The tone of the story need not be solemn. The darker aspects of life need not be ignored. But I think intimacy is indispensable—a feeling that derives from the listener's trust and a storyteller's certain knowledge of his subject and regard for his audience. This intimacy deepens if the storyteller tempers his authority with humility, or when terms of idiomatic expression, or at least the physical setting for the story, are shared.

I think of two landscapes—one outside the self, the other within. The external landscape is the one we see—not only the line and color of the land and its shading at different times of the day, but also its plants and animals in season, its weather, its geology, the record of its climate and evolution. If you walk up, say, a dry arroyo in the Sonoran Desert you will feel a mounding and rolling of sand and silt beneath your foot that is distinctive. You will anticipate the crumbling of the sedimentary earth in the arroyo bank as your hand reaches out, and in that tangible evidence you will sense a history of water in the region. Perhaps a black-throated sparrow lands in a paloverde bush—the resiliency of the twig under the bird, that precise shade of yellowish-green against the milk-blue sky, the fluttering whir of the arriving sparrow, are what I mean by "the landscape." Draw on the smell of creosote bush, or clack stones together in the dry air. Feel how light is the desiccated dropping of the kangaroo rat. Study an animal track obscured by the wind. These are all elements of the land, and what makes the landscape comprehensible are the relationships between them. One learns a landscape finally not by knowing the name or identity of everything in it, but by perceiving the relationships in it—like that between the sparrow and the twig. The difference between the relationships and the elements is the same as that between written history and a catalog of events.

The second landscape I think of is an interior one, a kind of projection within a person of a part of the exterior landscape. Relationships in the exterior landscape include those that are named and discernible, such as the nitrogen cycle, or a vertical sequence of Ordovician limestone, and others that are uncodified or ineffable, such as winter light falling on a particular kind of granite, or the effect of humidity on the frequency of a blackpoll warbler's burst of song. That these relationships have purpose and order, however inscrutable they may seem to us, is a tenet of evolution. Similarly, the speculations, intuitions, and formal ideas we refer to as "mind" are a set of relationships in the interior landscape with purpose and order; some of these are obvious, many impenetrably subtle. The shape and character of these relationships in a person's thinking, I believe, are deeply influenced by where on this earth one goes, what one touches, the patterns one observes in nature—the intricate history of one's life in the land, even a life in the city, where wind, the chirp of birds, the line of a falling leaf, are known. These thoughts are arranged, further, according to the thread of one's moral, intellectual, and spiritual development. The interior landscape responds to the character and subtlety of an exterior landscape; the shape of the individual mind is affected by land as it is by genes.

In stories like those I heard at Anaktuvuk Pass about wolverine, the relationship between separate elements in the land is set forth clearly. It is put in a simple framework of sequential incidents and apposite detail. If the exterior landscape is limned well, the listener often feels that he has heard something pleasing and authentic—trustworthy. We derive this sense of confidence I think not so much from verifiable truth as from an understanding that lying has played no role in the narrative. The storyteller is obligated to engage the reader with a precise vocabulary, to set forth a coherent and dramatic rendering of incidents—and to be ingenuous.

10 When one hears a story one takes pleasure in it for different reasons—for the euphony of its phrases, an aspect of the plot, or because one identifies with one of the characters. With certain stories certain individuals may experience a deeper, more profound sense of well-being. This latter phenomenon, in my understanding, rests at the heart of storytelling as an elevated experience among aboriginal peoples. It results from bringing two landscapes together. The exterior landscape is organized according to principles or laws or tendencies beyond human control. It is understood to contain an integrity that is beyond human analysis and unimpeachable. Insofar as the storyteller depicts various subtle and obvious relationships in the exterior landscape accurately in his story, and insofar as he orders them along traditional lines of meaning to create the narrative, the narrative will "ring true." The listener who "takes the story to heart" will feel a pervasive sense of congruence within himself and also with the world.

Among the Navajo and, as far as I know, many other native peoples, the land is thought to exhibit a sacred order. That order is the basis of ritual. The rituals themselves reveal the power in that order. Art, architecture, vocabulary, and costume, as well as ritual, are derived from the perceived natural order of the universe—from observations and meditations on the exterior landscape. An indigenous philosophy—metaphysics, ethics, epistemology, aesthetics, and logic—may also be derived from a people's continuous attentiveness to both the obvious (scientific) and ineffable (artistic) orders of the local landscape. Each individual, further, undertakes to order his interior landscape according to the exterior landscape. To succeed in this means to achieve a balanced state of mental health.

I think of the Navajo for a specific reason. Among the various sung ceremonies of this people—Enemyway, Coyoteway, Red Antway, Uglyway—is one called Beautyway. In the Navajo view, the elements of one's interior life—one's psychological makeup and moral bearing—are subject to a persistent principle of disarray. Beautyway is, in part, a spiritual invocation of the order of the exterior universe, that irreducible, holy complexity that manifests itself as all things changing through time (a Navajo definition of beauty, hózhǫ́ǫ́). The purpose of this invocation is to recreate in the individual who is the subject of the Beautyway ceremony that same order, to make the individual again a reflection of the myriad enduring relationships of the landscape.

I believe story functions in a similar way. A story draws on relationships in the exterior landscape and projects them onto the interior landscape. The purpose of storytelling is to achieve harmony between the two landscapes, to use all the elements of story—syntax, mood, figures of speech—in a harmonious way to reproduce the harmony of the land in the individual's interior. Inherent in story is the power to reorder a state of psychological confusion through contact with the pervasive truth of those relationships we call "the land."

These thoughts, of course, are susceptible to interpretation. I am convinced, however, that these observations can be applied to the kind of prose we call nonfiction as well as to traditional narrative forms such as the novel and the short story, and to some poems. Distinctions between fiction and nonfiction are sometimes obscured by arguments over what constitutes "the truth." In the aboriginal literature I am familiar with, the first distinction made among narratives is to separate the authentic from the inauthentic. Myth, which we tend to regard as fictitious or "merely metaphorical," is as authentic, as real, as the story of a wolverine in a man's lap. (A distinction is made, of course, about the elevated nature of myth—and frequently the circumstances of myth-telling are more rigorously prescribed than those for the telling of legends or vernacular stories—but all of these narratives are rooted in the local landscape. To violate *that* connection is to call the narrative itself into question.)

The power of narrative to nurture and heal, to repair a spirit in disarray, rests on two things: the skillful invocation of unimpeachable sources and a listener's knowledge that no hypocrisy or subterfuge is involved. This last simple fact is to me one of the most imposing aspects of the Holocene history of man.

We are more accustomed now to thinking of "the truth" as something that can be explicitly stated, rather than as something that can be evoked in a metaphorical way outside science and Occidental culture. Neither can truth be reduced to aphorism or formulas. It is something alive and unpronounceable. Story creates an atmosphere in which it becomes discernible as a pattern. For a storyteller to insist on relationships that do not exist is to lie. Lying is the opposite of story. (I do not mean to confuse ignorance with deception, or to imply that a storyteller can perceive all that is inherent in the land. Every storyteller falls short of a perfect limning of the landscape—perception and language both fail. But to make up something that is not there, something which can never be corroborated in the land, to knowingly set forth a false relationship, is to be lying, no longer telling a story.)

Because of the intricate, complex nature of the land, it is not always possible for a storyteller to grasp what is contained in a story. The intent of the storyteller, then, must be to evoke, honestly, some single aspect of all that the land contains. The storyteller knows that because different individuals grasp the story at different levels, the focus of his regard for truth must be at the primary one—with who was there, what happened, when, where, and why things occurred. The story will then possess similar truth at other levels—the integrity inherent at the primary level of meaning will be conveyed everywhere else. As long as the storyteller carefully describes the order before him, and uses his storytelling skill to heighten and emphasize certain relationships, it is even possible for the story to be more successful than the storyteller himself is able to imagine.

I would like to make a final point about the wolverine stories I heard at Anaktuvuk Pass. I wrote down the details afterward, concentrating especially on aspects of the biology and ecology of the animals.

I sent the information on to my friend living with the Cree. When, many months later, I saw him, I asked whether the Cree had enjoyed these insights of the Nunamiut into the nature of the wolverine. What had they said?

"You know," he told me, "how they are. They said, 'That could happen.' "

In these uncomplicated words the Cree declared their own knowledge of the wolverine. They acknowledged that although they themselves had never seen the things the Nunamiut spoke of, they accepted them as accurate observations, because they did not consider story a context for misrepresentation. They also preserved their own dignity by not overstating their confidence in the Nunamiut, a distant and unknown people.

Whenever I think of this courtesy on the part of the Cree I think of the dignity that is ours when we cease to demand the truth and realize that the best we can have of those substantial truths that guide our lives is metaphorical—a story. And the most of it we are likely to discern comes only when we accord one another the respect the Cree showed the Nunamiut. Beyond this—that the interior landscape is a metaphorical representation of the exterior landscape, that the truth reveals itself most fully not in dogma but in the paradox, irony, and contradictions that distinguish compelling narratives—beyond this there are only failures of imagination: reductionism in science; fundamentalism in religion; fascism in politics.

Our national literatures should be important to us insofar as they sustain us with illumination and heal us. They can always do that so long as they are written with respect for both the source and the reader, and with an understanding of why the human heart and the land have been brought together so regularly in human history.

Questions on Meaning

1. Why does Lopez say a story is able to affect us so powerfully only if "the story is told for its own sake, not forced to serve merely as the vehicle for an idea"? What would happen to the story if it were forced to become such a vehicle?
2. The essay repeatedly uses the word "heal" in reference to the power of storytelling for people. Explain what "heal" means in this context.
3. Describe the relationship between the external landscape and the internal landscape.

Questions on Rhetorical Strategy and Style

1. Lopez includes several different examples of people with storytelling traditions: the wolverine hunters, the Navajo, and the Cree. Analyze how these examples help the essay build its thesis.
2. Reread the story of the wolverine in the third paragraph. How does this simple story illustrate Lopez's point that storytelling should evoke something "that would never be completely understood" even as it helps shape our interior landscape and understanding of the world?
3. Lopez moves easily back and forth between the smallest details of physical landscape ("the resiliency of the twig under the bird, that precise shade of yellowish-green against the milk-blue sky") and large abstractions ("the speculations, intuitions, and formal ideas we refer to as 'mind' are a set of relationships in the interior landscape with purpose and order"). Does this style present you with any difficulties in the reading? How else could the essay have been written? How would its meaning and impact have changed? Explain your responses with examples from the essay.

Writing Assignments

1. Do you have a favorite experience that you enjoy telling about? Or do you remember a particular story you heard from a parent, relative, friend, or significant other? Analyze that story in terms of Lopez's ideas about the effects of storytelling: renewal of enthusiasm, a sense of self-being, healing, and different levels of meaning.

2. What natural landscape are you most familiar with? Sit in a quiet place with eyes closed and try to visualize that landscape in as much detail as you can. Let the picture fill itself in until you have a sense of actually being there. Now think of the words you would use to describe that landscape. Write a brief description. Analyze what you have written and see what glimpses into your own interior landscape emerge from the language you have used.
3. Write a short narrative of any surprising or interesting experience you have had recently. Try intentionally *not* to make a point with this story—try to let it speak for itself. Is it easier or more difficult to tell a story this way, compared to writing an essay with a clear point? How and why?

McBastards: McDonald's and Globalization

Paul Feine

Paul Feine is associated with the Centre for Civil Society and is a program director at aWorldConnected.org. This essay takes a friendly and casual look at the much-criticized McDonald's empire. Feine describes the trials of traveling in Paris with a small child who will not eat French food and who also annoys the French when he appears in their presence. In such circumstances, nothing is as good as a McDonald's french fry, or pommes frites as the French would say, for keeping a child quiet and happy. The American traveler sighs with relief at the sight of those arches and a hot Quarter-Pounder.

1 On a recent trip to Paris with my family, I was standing inside a 1
McDonald's restaurant gazing out at the street as my wife ordered Le Happy Meal for our two-year old. My son at the time was happily tugging away at my hair from his perch in his baby backpack (one of the most significant technological innovations in recent history, to my mind).

We hadn't traveled to Paris with the intention of eating at McDonald's, but we were looking for a quick fix for our hungry little boy, and McDonald's represented a cheap alternative to the more traditional cafés. Typical Paris cafés are not only far more expensive, but as previous experience made clear, they tend to be filled with Parisians who are less than charmed by the presence of toddlers.

As I pondered the differing cultural attitudes toward children and stared out onto the busy Paris street, my gaze rested on an elderly French man, whom I instantly categorized as quintessentially French,

---

Reprinted from *www.aworldconnected.org*, by permission of the author.

complete with black beret, long black trench coat, and a cane. The man hobbled by the entrance to McDonald's, stopped, turned to look inside, spat loudly, and sneered "bastards," or its rough equivalent in French.

I sipped my coffee, which was very good (Café Jacques Vabre, I learned later), while our son used his pommes frites as a ketchup delivery device and my wife drank from a bottle of Evian. We both chuckled as I shared with her the image of the authentic anti-McDonald's activist I had just witnessed.

McWhipping Boy

As the symbol for cultural imperialism and multinational corporate greed, McDonald's takes a lot of heat. *McSpotlight*, the anti-McDonald's website, for instance, boasts over one million hits per month. Critics demonize McDonald's for its unabashed pursuit of profits, its disregard for nutritional value and the environment, and the way it panders to children.

Most recently, McDonald's has been condemned for systematically seeking to addict naïve youngsters to its fatty fare, just like its evil older brothers in the cigarette business. In fact, crusading public interest lawyer John Banzhaf (whose van sports a license plate with a shortened version of "sue the bastards") is *suing McDonald's* in an attempt to hold them responsible for fast food addicts' health problems.

Indeed, though this multinational giant controls 43% of the US fast food market, the avarice of McDonald's seems to have no bounds. As Nick Gillespie of *Reason* magazine points out, "McDonald's is so desperate for customers that it's held prices essentially constant over the past two decades, while boosting portion sizes (burgers, fries, and drinks are all bigger than they used to be), expanding its menu, and building elaborate play structures for kids while simultaneously throwing increasingly sophisticated toys at them."

As anyone with small children knows, safe and secure McDonald's Playlands can be a dream come true, especially when you're stuck inside on a rainy day with kids who desperately need to burn some energy. Tiny plastic toys are received with as much delight as any large plastic toy they might have received last Christmas and, it must be emphasized, they're free.

Maybe, just maybe, McDonald's, in its unwavering pursuit of profits, has figured out the secret to succeeding in business—you've got to give the people what they want.

McCulture?

Okay, maybe McDonald's is fine for the U.S. Perhaps we're too value conscious, gluttonous, and superficial to care that our landscapes are littered with gleaming arches that have already polluted our bodies and our minds. But surely the same cannot be said for other societies around the world. Isn't it true that places that still have truly authentic dining experiences should be protected from the barbaric McHordes that are clamoring at their gates?

Golden Arches East, a recent book edited by James Watson, seeks to gain a better grasp on how McDonald's is affecting Asian culture. The results of this inquiry are in many ways surprising. For instance, one essay tells the story of an unintended and unanticipated consequence of McDonald's invasion of Hong Kong—the rest rooms in the city became cleaner.

Before the first McDonald's opened up in the mid-1970s, restaurant restrooms in Hong Kong were notoriously dirty. Over time, the cleanliness standards of McDonald's were replicated by other restaurants eager to out-compete the increasingly popular restaurant.

In Korea, McDonald's established the practice of lining up in an orderly fashion to order food—the traditional custom, it seems, was to mob the counter.

When the first McDonald's was opened in Moscow, it was necessary for an employee to stand outside the McDonald's with a blow horn in order to explain to those in the queue that the smiling employees were not laughing at them but, rather, were pleased to serve them.

Moreover, and in contradistinction to the widespread assumption that McDonald's is having an implacably homogenizing effect on global culture, *Golden Arches East* is filled with examples of the pains McDonald's takes to appeal to the unique local tastes and customs of people around the world. My own experience with the decidedly leisurely attitude of McDonald's employees in southern Spain further attests to McDonald's ability to adapt to the local culture.

Is It True That No Two Countries with McDonald's Have Ever Gone to War?

Long before I'd enjoyed the Andalucian version of McDonald's, I traveled to Belgrade, in what was then Yugoslavia, and I must admit that I was ecstatic to see a sign for a recently opened McDonald's. I'd just spent a couple of months consuming nothing but souvlaki, salad, and Ouzo in Greece, and the very thought of a Quarter-Pounder and a Coke made my mouth water.

My traveling buddy and I proceeded to wait in line for more than an hour and, as I stood happily munching on a french fry that brought back sweet memories of childhood Sunday-after-church treats, I looked across a sea of dark haired Yugoslavians into the eyes of two beautiful, blonde, obviously American women (actually it turned out they were Canadian nurses, but who am I to complain?). Absurdly, we waved to each other and fought through the crowd to greet one other like dear old friends. The memory of that day in Belgrade still brings a smile to my face.

Although you often hear people say it, it's not quite true that no two countries with McDonald's have ever gone to war—both the U.S. and Serbia, for example, had McDonald's during the conflict between the two nations. But even if McDonald's isn't a kind of multinational for-profit god of peace, McDonald's does provide cheap food, decent coffee, and free entertainment for kids, not to mention a salad-in-a-cup for health-conscious parents.

Around the world, this increasingly popular symbol (like it or not) of America is encouraging healthy competition—competition that, in many cases, is leading to improved sanitation standards and civility. And sometimes, just sometimes, McDonald's even brings people together and creates a few smiles . . . just like its commercials say it does.

The bastards.

Questions on Meaning

1. According to Feine, what is the attitude of the French toward small children and fast food? How does the Frenchman in the essay express that attitude?
2. The author says that it is true that McDonald's controls the food market and will do anything to keep that control, but it offers plastic toys and safe playgrounds. What does he say then matters most to a parent?
3. How does McDonald's adapt to the world cultures that it infiltrates? What is Feine's attitude towards that adaptation? What improvements does he claim that McDonald's has brought to the world?

Questions on Rhetorical Strategy and Style

1. This essay operates within a frame of two personal narratives, one recently when the author took his family to Paris and one in the past when he was a younger man. What did the experiences have in common? How does this frame help to make the point of the essay?
2. Within the humor of the essay is a solid point about the good that a big corporation can do when it is well run, as well as a second point that we live and travel looking for the familiar even in the strange. How does Feine illustrate these points?
3. The essay ends by saying that competition is healthy. How has Feine proved that McDonald's demonstrates "healthy" competition? Do you agree, and why?

Writing Assignments

1. Describe a time when familiar and comfortable food meant a lot to you when you were traveling or just sad and tired.
2. Visit a local McDonald's. Write about what you see. Who eats there? How many children are in the restaurant? What are they doing? What do you conclude from what you see? Write about your impressions.

3. When is competition good for people, and when does it become unhealthy? Use your own experiences to illustrate both perspectives in an essay on the value and danger of being competitive.

Building Plans: What the World Trade Center Meant

Paul Goldberger

Paul Goldberger (1950–) graduated from Yale University in 1972. He is a distinguished architectural critic and has taught at the Yale School of Architecture. In 1984, while writing for The New York Times, *he won the Pulitzer Prize in the commentary category for architectural criticism. Currently, he is the architectural critic at* The New Yorker. *He has authored numerous works, including* A Source Book of American Architecture *(2000). Fall 2004 will see the publication of* Up from Zero: Architecture, Politics, and the Rebuilding of New York, *a book dealing with the redevelopment of the World Trade Center site. The following essay was written for a special edition of* The New Yorker *that appeared on September 26, 2001.*

1 There have been skyscrapers in New York for more than a century, and we are accustomed to seeing the bigger, stronger buildings crowd out the smaller, weaker ones. Height is our most potent architectural currency. The Metropolitan Life campanile reigned once, then the Woolworth Building and, briefly, the Chrysler Building, then the Empire State Building and the World Trade Center towers, those two vertical lines that anchored the composition of the skyline for twenty-five years. The towers were not beautiful buildings. They were gargantuan and banal, blandness blown up to a gigan- 1

tic size. But size was the point, and the people who stood in line to visit the hundred-and-seventh-floor observation deck or eat at Windows on the World and buy little souvenir snow globes with the towers inside understood this, just as real-estate developers did, and as the terrorists who rammed their planes into the towers last week did.

With the invention of the passenger elevator in the mid-nineteenth century and the steel frame two decades later, an intimate connection was forged between the tallest tower in the city and the biggest corporation, the richest bank, or whatever financial entity wanted to be seen as running the place. Before there were skyscrapers, the horizon in most cities was dominated by church steeples. (In New York, the tallest thing was Richard Upjohn's Trinity Church, built in 1846.) The earliest skyscrapers wrested control of the skyline from God and gave it to Mammon, where it has pretty much remained. In 1913, a fawning minister called the Woolworth Building the "cathedral of commerce," in celebration of the triumph of corporate power that Cass Gilbert's lyrical Gothic skyscraper represented. It is a pretty straight line from the Woolworth Building to the World Trade Center. The architectural dressing changed, but the basic idea of building as high as you could to express power became a convention in almost every city, first in this country and then, by the nineteen-eighties, around the world.

The urge to make buildings higher and higher has been fading for the last few years, for purely practical reasons. Constructing towers of a hundred stories or more isn't much of a challenge technologically today, but it is not particularly economical, either. It never was. The space on the lower floors that is given up to make room for elevator shafts to the upper floors cuts into rentable space. The World Trade Center was a dinosaur in this sense, although the economics of the place got a lot better over time, and just two months ago the Port Authority concluded a deal to least the towers for $3.2 billion to the developer Larry Silverstein, who then hired David Childs, of Skidmore, Owings & Merrill, to upgrade the complex. Childs has designed several new towers in New York, including the A.O.L. Time Warner Center that is going up at Columbus Circle. Silverstein hoped to fix up the Trade Center's image and turn it into a kind of downtown Rockefeller Center.

The very tallest buildings have usually been put up by people more interested in attention-getting value than in immediate financial return. That was the motivation of Governor Nelson Rockefeller and the Port Authority in the nineteen-sixties, when the World Trade Center was conceived, and it is the motivation for the entrepreneurs who have built or plan to build tall buildings in cities like Shanghai, Hong Kong, and Kuala Lumpur, where the Petronas Towers, the tallest skyscrapers in the world at the moment, were built in 1998. The destruction of the World Trade Center may well put an end to this kind of thing. "I think many of our clients would not want to build such a visible symbol, that they will want to build not so iconic and not so tall, the way the wealthy in Mexico started driving around in Volkswagens instead of Jaguars," David Childs said a few days ago.

5 The Trade Center was structurally innovative. Earlier skyscrapers were supported by complex frames of steel or concrete columns and beams. Their exteriors were a "curtain wall" of metal, glass, or masonry hung from the frame, and their interiors were broken up by the grid of columns and beams. The Trade Center was more like a vast tube. Its exterior walls were a kind of steel mesh that supported most of the building's structural weight, freeing the interior floors from the usual maze of columns. The architects, Minoru Yamasaki and Emery Roth & Sons, and the engineer, Leslie Robertson, did not invent this tubular system. It was used earlier by Fazlur Khan and Myron Goldsmith, of Skidmore, Owings & Merrill, for an apartment house in Chicago finished in 1965. But the use of it at the Trade Center towers, which at the time of their construction were the tallest buildings in the world, represented an enormous advance. It was part of a tendency toward lightness in the design of almost everything—from cars and telephones to buildings.

Lighter does not mean weaker, of course. The relative lightness of the twin towers compared with, say, the Empire State Building, which has a steel frame and limestone cladding, does not appear to have been a factor in their collapse. Nothing about the design of the buildings seems to be intrinsically at fault. The towers withstood the assaults. They did not fall over, and their tops did not slice off. It was the explosions of the jet fuel that did the buildings in, not the impact of the jetliners themselves, and the buildings did not collapse until some time after the crashes—well over an hour for one tower, just under an hour for the other. Steel softens and melts under tremendous heat—it is, after all, created by the heat of the forge—and it was only a matter of time before the extraordinary heat of the fire would take its toll.

The Trade Center was "amazingly robust," said Bill Baker, an engineer at the Skidmore firm who has designed the structural systems for several new skyscrapers. "It took a large commercial jet and the explosion, and it still stood, which is a lot to ask of any building." Fireproofing, Baker explained, "is really just a matter of buying time, and the building did buy time. There was basically an hour and forty minutes, and while a lot of people didn't make it out, a lot of people did."

The structural system of a skyscraper is designed to support the mass of the building itself—so that it does not collapse of its own weight—and to protect it from natural forces such as earthquakes and wind. Wind affects every skyscraper. The taller a building is, the greater the forces of wind pummeling it. Engineers have become so good at handling this that buildings don't fall down and they don't usually sway noticeably, either. But there isn't any building, except maybe the Pyramids, that could withstand the consequences of an enormous jetliner smashing into it with a full load of fuel. "You can't design for that, just like you can't design for the epicenter of an earthquake," David Childs said. William Pedersen, of Kohn Pedersen Fox, the architect of the new financial center planned for Shanghai, which would be slightly taller than the towers in Kuala Lumpur, says that when his firm was designing that building, there were no discussions of planes fully loaded with fuel flying into it. "If there is a physical way to protect a building from this, which I doubt, it would be prohibitive in cost, and the natural light would disappear."

Architecture doesn't usually work symbolically until it has been around for a while. The Woolworth Building went up less than a decade after the Wright Brothers took their first flight at Kitty Hawk. It still stands, just a few blocks to the east of the site of the World Trade Center, and it looked tiny in the televised shots of lower Manhattan last week, a delicate, dignified artifact.

Many of our greatest urban symbols achieve their meaning by connecting monumentality with the business of everyday life. Unlike cities such as Washington, D.C., New York has few pure monuments, with no purpose other than to inspire. There is the Statue of Liberty, but almost every other symbol of New York combines architectural ambition with the prosaic. People drive and walk across the Brooklyn Bridge every day. They ride their bicycles in Central Park, they board trains at Grand Central, and they go to work in Rockefeller Center or the Empire State Building. The Eiffel Tower is vastly more beautiful than the Trade Center was—so, for that matter, is the Empire State Building—but it is not part of life in Paris in quite the same way that the skyscrapers are part of life in New York. When the Eiffel Tower was built, a gaggle of artists and writers protested that it had nothing to do with Paris. No one could make that point about our skyscrapers. They were part of the city's essence from the day they went up.

We count on our urban symbols to be present. They are not supposed to evaporate. When buildings go away, they go almost as slowly as they came, piece by piece. The architect Cesar Pelli estimates that if the World Trade Center had been demolished conventionally it would have taken two years to dismantle. Pelli, who designed the World Financial Center, four squat towers next to the Trade Center, said to me that he thought of his buildings as "a set of foothills beside the mountain, and now the mountain is gone." It was an enormous familiar presence. As the years passed, it seemed to take on the quality of a huge piece of minimalist sculpture, and its dullness was almost a virtue. Now that the Trade Center has become a martyr to terrorism, I suspect that architectural criticism of it will cease altogether. It has become a noble monument of a lost past. It is no more possible to know what will replace it as a symbol than it is to know what, if anything, will be built someday where the towers stood. But when the biggest thing in a city that prizes bigness becomes the most fragile thing, and the void has more weight than the solid, the rules of city-building change.

Questions on Meaning

1. What were the aspects of the World Trade Center that made it "structurally innovative," as the author says? Why was the design significant and how are its concepts still applied to other technologies?
2. A skyscraper is not just a tall building. How did the development of the skyscraper signal a shift in the social and economic conditions of its time?
3. What does the author mean by the statement, "Architecture doesn't usually work symbolically until it has been around for a while"? What conditions and characteristics are required for a piece of architecture to take on symbolic significance?

Questions on Rhetorical Strategy and Style

1. While the essay is about a tragic event, the author manages to approach his subject objectively. How did you respond to this? Why might it have been important to use a critical tone? Identify the instances where the more lyrical statements are made.
2. Why does the author provide readers with the brief history of skyscrapers in New York? How does this provide context for discussing the significance of the World Trade Center? Why does he speculate on the future of architecture?
3. On the surface, the essay appears prosaic. Still, the author is making an argument. Where are his intentions revealed? What does he want his readers to think or believe?

Writing Assignments

1. The author stresses that, in one respect, the structural engineering of towers did not fail. At the time of the terrorist attack many felt compelled to point this out. While this is no doubt true, subsequent reports suggested that the fireproofing on the beams was inadequate, which may have caused the steel to melt faster. Also, some feel that had the stairwells been wider and better insulated, more people could have escaped. Conduct your own research on the reports on the destruction of the towers and write your own review of what they conclude.

2. Analyze the plans for rebuilding the World Trade Center site. Write an essay in which you respond to these plans and the controversies surrounding them. How will the plans reestablish the site's economic significance while, at the same time, memorialize the events of September 11, 2001?

The Beatles: They Changed Rock, Which Changed the Culture, Which Changed US

Jeff Greenfield

Jeff Greenfield (1943–) was born in New York City. A graduate of the University of Wisconsin and Yale University School of Law, he has worked as legislative aide and speechwriter (notably for former New York City Mayor John Lindsay and for the late Senator Robert Kennedy), a television correspondent and commentator for ABC, and a syndicated columnist. His books, which frequently focus on sports, politics, and the media, include Where Have You Gone, Joe DiMaggio? *(1973),* The World's Greatest Team: A Portrait of the Boston Celtics *(1976),* Television: The First Fifty Years *(1977),* Playing to Win: An Insider's Guide to Politics *(1980),* The Real Campaign: How the Media Missed the Story of the 1980 Campaign *(1982), and* The People's Choice *(1995). He also coauthored (with Jack Newfield)* A Populist Manifesto *(1972). Greenfield contemplates the impact of the Beatles on rock, culture, and a large generation of "baby boomers" in this 1975 essay. As you read, try to identify another popular person or group that has had a similar impact on your life.*

1 They have not performed together on stage for more than eight years. They have not made a record together in five years. The formal dissolution of their partnership in a London courtroom last month was an echo of an ending that came long ago. Now each of them is seeking to overcome the shadow of a past in which

they were bound together by wealth, fame and adulation of an intensity unequaled in our culture. George Harrison scorns talk of reunion, telling us to stop living in the past. John Lennon told us years ago that "the dream is over."

He was right: When the Beatles broke up in 1970 in a welter of lawsuits and recriminations, the sixties were ending as well—in spirit as well as by the calendar. Bloodshed and bombings on campus, the harsh realities beneath the facile hopes for a "Woodstock nation," the shabby refuse of counterculture communities, all helped kill the dream.

What remains remarkable now, almost 20 years after John Lennon started playing rock 'n' roll music, more than a decade after their first worldwide conquest, is how appealing this dream was: how its vision of the world gripped so much of a generation; how that dream reshaped our recent past and affects us still. What remains remarkable is how strongly this dream was triggered, nurtured and broadened by one rock 'n' roll band of four Englishmen whose entire history as a group occurred before any of them reached the age of 30.

Their very power guarantees that an excursion into analysis cannot fully succeed. Their songs, their films, their lives formed so great a part of what we listened to and watched and talked about that everyone affected by them still sees the Beatles and hears their songs through a personal prism. And the Beatles themselves never abandoned a sense of self-parody and put-on. They were, in Richard Goldstein's phrase, "the clown-gurus of the sixties." Lennon said more than once that the Beatles sometimes put elusive references into their songs just to confuse their more solemn interpreters. "I am the egg man," they sang, not "egghead."

Still, the impact of the Beatles cannot be waved away. If the Marx they emulated was Groucho, not Karl, if their world was a playground instead of a battleground, they still changed what we listened to and how we listened to it; they helped make rock music a battering ram for the youth culture's assault on the mainstream, and that assault in turn changed our culture permanently. And if the "dream" the Beatles helped create could not sustain itself in the real world, that speaks more to our false hopes than to their promises. They wrote and sang songs. We turned it into politics and philosophy and a road map to another way of life. The Beatles grew up as children of the first generation of rock 'n' roll, listening to and imitating the music of Little

Richard, Larry Williams, Chuck Berry, Elvis Presley, and the later, more sophisticated sounds of the Shirelles and the Miracles. It was the special genius of their first mentor, Brian Epstein, to package four Liverpool working-class "rockers" as "mods," replacing their greasy hair, leather jackets, and onstage vulgarity with jackets, ties, smiles and carefully groomed, distinctive haircuts. Just as white artists filtered and softened the raw energy of black artists in the nineteen-fifties, the Beatles at first were softer, safer versions of energetic rock 'n' roll musicians. The words promised they only wanted to hold hands—the rhythm was more insistent.

By coming into prominence early in 1964, the Beatles probably saved rock 'n' roll from extinction. Rock in the early nineteen-sixties existed in name only; apart from the soul artists, it was a time of "shlock rock," with talentless media hypes like Fabian and Frankie Avalon riding the crest of the American Bandstand wave. By contrast, the Beatles provided a sense of musical energy that made successful a brilliant public-relations effort. Of course, the $50,000 used to promote the Beatles' first American appearance in February, 1964, fueled some of the early hysteria; so did the timing of their arrival.

Coming as it did less than a hundred days after the murder of John Kennedy, the advent of the Beatles caught America aching for any diversion to replace the images of a flag-draped casket and a riderless horse in the streets of Washington.

I remember a Sunday evening in early February, standing with hundreds of curious collegians in a University of Wisconsin dormitory, watching these four longhaired (!) Englishmen trying to be heard over the screams of Ed Sullivan's audience. Their music seemed to me then derivative, pleasant and bland, a mixture of hard rock and the sounds of the black groups then popular. I was convinced it would last six months, no more.

The Beatles, however, had more than hype; they had talent. Even their first hits, "I Want to Hold Your Hand," "She Loves You," "Please Please Me," "I Saw Her Standing There," had a hint of harmonies and melodies more inventive than standard rock tunes. More important, it became immediately clear that the Beatles were hipper, more complicated, than the bovine rock stars who could not seem to put four coherent words together.

10 In the spring of 1964, John Lennon published a book, "In His Own Write," which, instead of a ghost-written string of "groovy

guides for keen teens," offered word plays, puns and black-humor satirical sketches. A few months later came the film "A Hard Day's Night," and in place of the classic let's-put-on-a-prom-and-invite-the-TeenChords plot of rock movies, the Beatles and director Richard Lester created a funny movie parodying the Beatles's own image.

I vividly recall going to that film in the midst of a National Student Association Congress: at that time, rock 'n' roll was regarded as high-school nonsense by this solemn band of student-body presidents and future C.I.A. operatives. But after the film, I sensed a feeling of goodwill and camaraderie among that handful of rock fans who had watched this movie: The Beatles were media heroes without illusion, young men glorying in their sense of play and fun, laughing at the conventions of the world. They were worth listening to and admiring.

The real surprise came at the end of 1965, with the release of the "Rubber Soul" album. Starting with that album, and continuing through "Revolver" and "Sgt. Pepper's Lonely Hearts Club Band," the Beatles began to throw away the rigid conventions of rock 'n' roll music and lyrics. The banal abstract, second-hand emotions were replaced with sharp, sometimes mordant portraits of first-hand people and experiences, linked to music that was more complicated and more compelling than rock had ever dared attempt. The Beatles were drawing on their memories and feelings, not those cut from Tin Pan Alley cloth.

"Norwegian Wood" was about an unhappy, inconclusive affair ("I once had a girl/or should I say/she once had me"). "Michelle" and "Yesterday" were haunting, sentimental ballads, and Paul McCartney dared sing part of "Michelle" in French—most rock singers regarded English as a foreign language. "Penny Lane" used cornets to evoke the suggestion of a faintly heard band concert on a long-ago summer day. Staccato strings lent urgency to the story of "Eleanor Rigby."

These songs were different from the rock music that our elders had scorned with impunity. Traditionally, rock 'n' roll was rigidly structured: 4/4 tempo, 32 bars, with a limited range of instruments. Before the Beatles, rock producer Phil Spector had revolutionized records by adding strings to the drums, bass, sax and guitar, but the chord structure was usually limited to a basic blues or ballad pattern. Now the Beatles, with the kind of visibility that made them impossible to ignore, were expanding the range of rock, musically and lyrically. A sitar—a harpsichord effect—a ragtime piano—everything was possible.

15 With the release of "Sgt. Pepper" in the spring of 1967, the era of rock as a strictly adolescent phenomenon was gone. One song, "A Day in the Life," with its recital of an ordinary day combined with a dreamlike sense of dread and anxiety, made it impossible to ignore the skills of Lennon and McCartney. A decade earlier, Steve Allen mocked the inanity of rock by reading "Hound Dog" or "Tutti-Frutti" as if they were serious attempts at poetry. Once "Sgt. Pepper" was recorded, *Partisan Review* was lauding the Beatles, Ned Rorem proclaimed that "She's Leaving Home" was "equal to any song Schubert ever wrote," and a *Newsweek* critic meant it when he wrote: " 'Strawberry Fields Forever' [is] a superb Beatleizing of hope and despair in which the four minstrels regretfully recommend a Keatsian lotus-land of withdrawal from the centrifugal stresses of the age."

"We're so well established," McCartney had said in 1966, "that we can bring fans along with us and stretch the limits of pop." By using their fame to help break through the boundaries of rock, the Beatles proved that they were not the puppets of backstage manipulation or payola or hysterical 14-year-olds. Instead, they helped make rock music *the* music of an entire international generation. Perhaps for the first time in history, it was possible to say that tens of millions of people, defined simply by age, were all doing the same thing: they were listening to rock 'n' roll. That fact changed the popular culture of the world.

Rock 'n' roll's popularity had never been accompanied by respectability, even among the young. For those of us with intellectual pretenses, rock 'n' roll was like masturbation: exciting, but shameful. The culturally alienated went in for cool jazz, and folk music was the vehicle for the politically active minority. (The growth of political interest at the start of the sixties sparked something of a folk revival.)

Along with the leap of Bob Dylan into rock music, the Beatles destroyed this division. Rock 'n' roll was now broad enough, free enough, to encompass every kind of feeling. Its strength had always been rooted in the sexual energy of its rhythms; in that sense, the outraged parents who had seen rock as a threat to their children's virtue were right. Rock 'n' roll made you want to move and shake and get physically excited. The Beatles proved that this energy could be fused with a sensibility more subtle than the "let's-go-down-to-the-gym-and-beat-up-the-Coke-machine" quality of rock music.

In 1965, Barry McGuire recorded the first "rock protest" song (excluding the teen complaints of the Coasters and Chuck Berry). In his "Eve of Destruction," we heard references to Red China, Selma, Alabama, nuclear war and middle-class hypocrisy pounded out to heavy rock rythms. That same year came a flood of "good time" rock music, with sweet, haunting melodies by groups like the Lovin' Spoonful and the Mamas and the Papas. There *were* no limits to what could be done; and the market was continually expanding.

The teenagers of the nineteen-fifties had become the young adults of the nineteen-sixties, entering the professions, bringing with them a cultural frame of reference shaped in good measure by rock 'n' roll. The "youth" market was enormous—the flood of babies born during and just after World War II made the under-25 population group abnormally large; their tastes were more influential than ever before. And because the music had won acceptability, rock 'n' roll was not judged indulgently as a "boys will be boys" fad. Rock music was expressing a sensibility about the tangible world—about sensuality, about colors and sensations, about the need to change consciousness. And this sensibility soon spilled over into other arenas.

Looking back on the last half of the last decade, it is hard to think of a cultural innovation that did not carry with it the influence of rock music, and of the Beatles in particular: the miniskirt, discothèques, the graphics of Peter Max, the birth of publications like *Rolling Stone,* the "mindbending" effects of TV commercials, the success of "Laugh-In" on television and "Easy Rider" in the movies—all of these cultural milestones owe something to the emergence of rock music as the most compelling and pervasive force in our culture.

This is especially true of the incredible spread of drugs—marijuana and the hallucinogens most particularly—among the youth culture. From "Rubber Soul" through "Sgt. Pepper," Beatle music was suffused with a sense of mystery and mysticism: odd choral progressions, mysterious instruments, dreamlike effects, and images that did not seem to yield to "straight" interpretation. Whether specific songs ("Lucy in the Sky with Diamonds," "A Little Help From My Friends") were deliberately referring to drugs is beside the point. The Beatles were publicly recounting their LSD experiences, and their music was replete with antirational sensibility. Indeed, it was a commonplace among my contemporaries that Beatle albums could not be understood fully without the use of drugs. For "Rubber Soul," marijuana; for "Sgt. Pepper," acid. When the Beatles told us to turn off our minds and float downstream, uncounted youngsters assumed that the key to this kind of mind-expansion could be found in a plant or a pill. Together with "head" groups like Jefferson Airplane and the Grateful Dead, the Beatles were, consciously or not, a major influence behind the spread of drugs.

In this sense, the Beatles are part of a chain: (1) the Beatles opened up rock; (2) rock changed the culture; (3) the culture changed us. Even limited to their impact as musicians, however, the Beatles were as powerful an influence as any group or individual; only Bob Dylan stands as their equal. They never stayed with a successful formula; they were always moving. By virtue of their fame, the Beatles were a giant amplifier, spreading "the word" on virtually every trend and mood of the last decade.

They were never pure forerunners. The Yardbirds used the sitar before the Beatles; the Beach Boys were experimenting with studio enhancement first; the Four Seasons were using elaborate harmonies before the Beatles. They were never as contemptuously antimiddle-class or decadent as the Kinks or the Rolling Stones; never as lyrically compelling as Dylan; never as musically brilliant as the Band; never as hallucinogenic as the San Francisco groups. John Gabree, one of the most perceptive of the early rock writers, said that "their job, and they have done it well, has been to travel a few miles behind the avant-garde, consolidating gains and popularizing new ideas."

Yet this very willingness meant that new ideas did not struggle and die in obscurity; instead, they touched a hundred million minds. Their songs reflected the widest range of mood of any group of their time. Their openness created a kind of salon for a whole generation of people, idea exchange into which the youth of the world was wired. It was almost inevitable that, even against their will, their listeners shaped a dream of politics and lifestyle from the substance of popular music. It is testament both to the power of rock music, and to the illusions which can be spun out of impulses.

The Beatles were not political animals. Whatever they have done since going their separate ways, their behavior as a group reflected cheerful anarchy more than political rebellion. Indeed, as editorialists, they were closer to *The Wall Street Journal* than to *Ramparts.* "Taxman" assaults the heavy progressive income tax ("one for you, 19 for me"), and "Revolution" warned that "if you go carrying pictures of Chairman Mao/you ain't gonna make it with anyone anyhow."

The real political impact of the Beatles was not in any four-point program or in an attack on injustice or the war in Vietnam. It was instead in the counterculture they had helped to create. Somewhere in the nineteen-sixties, millions of people began to regard themselves as a class separate from mainstream society *by virtue of their youth and the sensibility that youth produced.*

The nineteen-fifties had produced the faintest hint of such an attitude in the defensive love of rock 'n' roll; if our parents hated it, it had to be good. The sixties had expanded this vague idea into a battle cry. "Don't trust anyone over 30!"—shouted from a police car in the first massive student protest of the decade at Berkeley—suggested an outlook in which the mere aging process was an act of betrayal in which youth itself was a moral value. *Time* magazine made the "under-25 generation" its Man of the Year in 1967, and politicians saw in the steadily escalating rebellion among the middle-class young a constituency and a scapegoat.

The core value of this "class" was not peace or social injustice; it was instead a more elusive value, reflected by much of the music and by the Beatles' own portrait of themselves. It is expressed best by a scene from their movie "Help!" in which John, Paul, George and Ringo enter four adjoining row houses. The doors open—and suddenly the scene shifts inside, and we see that these "houses" are in fact one huge house; the four Beatles instantly reunite.

It is this sense of commonality that was at the heart of the youth culture. It is what we wished to believe about the Beatles, and about the possibilities in our own lives. If there is one sweeping statement that makes sense about the children of the last decade, it is that the generation born of World War II was saying "no" to the atomized lives their parents had so feverishly sought. The most cherished value of the counterculture—preached if not always practiced—was its insistence on sharing, communality, a rejection of the retreat into private satisfaction. Rock 'n' roll was the magnet, the driving force, of a shared celebration. From Alan Freed's first mammoth dance parties in Cleveland in 1951, to the Avalon Ballroom in San Francisco, to the be-ins in our big cities, to Woodstock itself. Spontaneous gathering was the ethic: Don't plan it, don't think about it, *do* it—you'll get by with a little help from your friends.

In their music, their films, their sense of play, the Beatles reflected this dream of a ceaseless celebration. If there *was* any real "message" in their songs, it was the message of Charles Reich: that the world would be changed by changing the consciousness of the new generation. "All you need is love," they sang. "Say the word [love] and you'll be free." "Let it be." "Everything's gonna be all right."

As a state of mind, it was a pleasant fantasy. As a way of life, it was doomed to disaster. The thousands of young people who flocked to California or to New York's Lower East Side to join the love generation found the world filled with people who did not share the ethic of mutual trust. The politicization of youth as a class helped to divide natural political allies and make politics more vulnerable to demagogues. As the Beatles found in their own personal and professional lives, the practical outside world has a merciless habit of intruding into fantasies; somebody has to pay the bills and somebody has to do the dishes in the commune and somebody has to protect us from the worst instincts of other human beings. John Lennon was expressing some very painful lessons when he told *Rolling Stone* shortly after the group's breakup that "nothing happened except we all dressed up . . . the same bastards are in control, the same people are runnin' everything."

Questions on Meaning

1. What were the dates of the following events in Beatles history: First American tour, last stage performance, last record together, breakup?
2. What does Greenfield mean by the "Woodstock nation" and the "sense of communality that was at the heart of the youth culture"? What was the role of rock 'n' roll in these movements?
3. Why does Greenfield say that the Beatles "probably saved rock 'n' roll from extinction"? Do you agree with that assertion? What do you think would have happened to rock if the Beatles had never happened?

Questions on Rhetorical Strategy and Style

1. Find where Greenfield uses a writing strategy of cause and effect to show how rock changed the culture. What examples of products and activities does he give to illustrate the influence of rock music on society?
2. Greenfield assumes that the reader has a certain knowledge of the Beatles and the era in which they performed. For instance, he only gives the names of two members of the group, and he does not identify a number of other persons he mentions, such as Brian Epstein, Ed Sullivan, and Charles Reich. How has this casual style held up decades after the essay was written? If Greenfield were to revise this essay, where would you like him to fill in details?
3. Do you agree with the title of this essay? How persuasive is Greenfield's argument? Reread the essay and mark the strong and weak points of his argument. Where applicable, indicate current societal icons who have had the same impact on your life as the Beatles seemed to have had on Greenfield.

Writing Assignments

1. Greenfield comments that everyone affected by the Beatles "hears their songs through a personal prism." Although he was referring to the generation that traveled through their teens and early 20s with the Beatles, the influence of this group has continued for following generations of youths. Describe the Beatles through your own "personal prism." How did you "Meet the Beatles" (the title of their first album)? What age were you when you began to

recognize their music? What role did their music play in the development of your musical preferences?

2. Greenfield contends "only Bob Dylan stands as their equal." Compare and contrast the impact of the Beatles and Dylan on the generation of youths who spent their formative years listening to their music. Consider their lyrics, their messages, their personas, and their musical styles. How have they weathered time?
3. Write an essay about the importance of cultural "icons" to young people. Compare and contrast how a person or group that appeals to youth both gives them a feeling of community and helps them develop their individuality. Provide examples of recent "icons" and describe their influence on music, reading, leisure activities, political views, and relationships. What is the response of adult mainstream America to these individuals or groups?

The Obligation to Endure

Rachel Carson

Rachel Carson (1907–1964), a pioneer of the environmental movement, was born in Pennsylvania. A naturalist by training, she specialized in marine biology and developed a particular affection for the rocky coast of Maine. Her seminal book Silent Spring *(1962), resulted from her work as an aquatic biologist for the U.S. Fish and Wildlife service, during which she became acutely aware of the ecological hazards of herbicides and insecticides. She also wrote* The Sea Around Us *(1951), for which she received the National Book Award,* Under the Sea Wind *(1952), and* The Edge of the Sea *(1955). Although Carson's writing was not without controversy, and for many years she was criticized as being an alarmist, she is now credited with being one of America's most important environmentalists. In this classic essay, Carson clearly implicates chemical pollutants—and people's careless use of them—in the degradation of the environment.*

1 The history of life on earth has been a history of interaction between living things and their surroundings. To a large extent, the physical form and the habits of the earth's vegetation and its animal life have been molded by the environment. Considering the whole span of earthly time, the opposite effect, in which life actually modifies its surroundings, has been relatively slight. Only within the moment of time represented by the present century has one species—man—acquired significant power to alter the nature of his world. 1

During the past quarter century this power has not only increased to one of disturbing magnitude but it has changed in character. The most alarming of all man's assaults upon the environment is the contamination of air, earth, rivers, and sea with dangerous and even lethal materials. This pollution is for the most part irrecoverable; the chain of evil it initiates not only in the world that must support life but in living tissues is for the most part irreversible. In this now universal contamination of the environment, chemicals are the sinister and little-recognized partners of radiation in changing the very nature of the world—the very nature of its life. Strontium 90, released through nuclear explosions into the air, comes to earth in rain or drifts down in fallout, lodges in soil, enters into the grass or corn or wheat grown there, and in time takes up its abode in the bones of a human being, there to remain until his death. Similarly, chemicals sprayed on croplands or forests or gardens lie long in soil, entering into living organisms, passing from one to another in a chain of poisoning and death. Or they pass mysteriously by underground streams until they emerge and, through the alchemy of air and sunlight, combine into new forms that kill vegetation, sicken cattle, and work unknown harm on those who drink from once pure wells. As Albert Schweitzer has said, "Man can hardly even recognize the devils of his own creation."

It took hundreds of millions of years to produce the life that now inhabits the earth—eons of time in which that developing and evolving and diversifying life reached a state of adjustment and balance with its surroundings. The environment, rigorously shaping and directing the life it supported, contained elements that were hostile as well as supporting. Certain rocks gave out dangerous radiation; even within the light of the sun, from which all life draws its energy, there were shortwave radiations with power to injure. Given time—time not in years but in millennia—life adjusts, and a balance has been reached. For time is the essential ingredient; but in the modern world there is no time.

The rapidity of change and the speed with which new situations are created follow the impetuous and heedless pace of man rather than the deliberate pace of nature. Radiation is no longer merely the background radiation of rocks, the bombardment of cosmic rays, the ultraviolet of the sun that have existed before there was any life on earth; radiation is now the unnatural creation of man's tampering with the atom. The chemicals to which life is asked to make its adjustment are no longer merely the calcium and silica and copper and all the rest of the minerals washed out of the rocks and carried in rivers to the sea; they are the synthetic creations of man's inventive mind, brewed in his laboratories, and having no counterparts in nature.

To adjust to these chemicals would require time on the scale that is nature's; it would require not merely the years of a man's life but the life of generations. And even this, were it by some miracle possible, would be futile, for the new chemicals come from our laboratories in an endless stream; almost five hundred annually find their way into actual use in the United States alone. The figure is staggering and its implications are not easily grasped—500 new chemicals to which the bodies of men and animals are required somehow to adapt each year, chemically totally outside the limits of biologic experience.

Among them are many that are used in man's war against nature. Since the mid-1940s over 200 basic chemicals have been created for use in killing insects, weeds, rodents, and other organisms described in the modern vernacular as "pests"; and they are sold under several thousand different brand names.

These sprays, dusts, and aerosols are now applied almost universally to farms, gardens, forests, and homes—nonselective chemicals that have the power to kill every insect, the "good" and the "bad," to still the songs of birds and the leaping of fish in the streams, to coat the leaves with a deadly film, and to linger on in soil—all this though the intended target may be only a few weeds or insects. Can anyone believe it is possible to lay down such a barrage of poisons on the surface of the earth without making it unfit for all life? They should not be called "insecticides," but "biocides."

The whole process of spraying seems caught up in an endless spiral. Since DDT was released for civilian use, a process of escalation has been going on in which ever more toxic materials must be found. This has happened because insects, in a triumphant vindication of Darwin's principle of the survival of the fittest, have evolved super races immune to the particular insecticide used, hence a deadlier one has always to be developed—and then a deadlier one than that. It has happened also because, for reasons to be described later, destructive insects often undergo a "flare-back" or resurgence, after spraying in numbers greater than before. Thus the chemical war is never won, and all life is caught in its violent crossfire.

Along with the possibility of the extinction of mankind by nuclear war, the central problem of our age has therefore become the contamination of man's total environment with such substances of incredible potential for harm—substances that accumulate in the tissues of plants and animals and even penetrate the germ cells to shatter or alter the very material of heredity upon which the shape of the future depends. Some would-be architects of our future look toward a time when it will be possible to alter the human germ plasm by design. But we may easily be doing so now by inadvertence, for many chemicals, like radiation, bring about gene mutations. It is ironic to think that man might determine his own future by something so seemingly trivial as the choice of an insect spray.

All this has been risked—for what? Future historians may well be amazed by our distorted sense of proportion. How could intelligent beings seek to control a few unwanted species by a method that contaminated the entire environment and brought the threat of disease and death even to their own kind? Yet this is precisely what we have done. We have done it, moreover, for reasons that collapse the moment we examine them. We are told that the enormous and expanding use of pesticides is necessary to maintain farm production. Yet is our real problem not one of *overproduction?* Our farms, despite measures to remove acreages from production and to pay farmers *not* to produce, have yielded such a staggering excess of crops that the American taxpayer in 1962 paid out more than one billion dollars a year as the total carrying cost of the surplus-food storage program. And is the situation helped when one branch of the Agriculture Department tries to reduce production while another states, as it did in 1958, "It is believed generally that reduction of crop acreages under provisions of the Soil Bank will stimulate interest in use of chemicals to obtain maximum production on the land retained in crops."

All this is not to say there is no insect problem and no need of control. I am saying, rather, that control must be geared to realities, not to mythical situations, and that the methods employed must be such that they do not destroy us along with the insects.

The problem whose attempted solution has brought such a train of disaster in its wake is an accomplishment of our modern way of life. Long before the age of man, insects inhabited the earth—a group of extraordinarily varied and adaptable beings. Over the course of time since man's advent, a small percentage of the more than half a million species of insects have come into conflict with human welfare in two principal ways: as competitors for the food supply and as carriers of human disease.

Disease-carrying insects become important where human beings are crowded together, especially under conditions where sanitation is poor, as in time of natural disaster or war or in situations of extreme poverty and deprivation. Then control of some sort becomes necessary. It is a sobering fact, however, as we shall presently see, that the method of massive chemical control has had only limited success, and also threatens to worsen the very conditions it is intended to curb.

Under primitive agricultural conditions the farmer had few insect problems. These arose with the intensification of agriculture—the devotion of immense acreages to a single crop. Such a system set the stage for explosive increases in specific insect populations. Single-crop farming does not take advantage of the principles by which nature works; it is agriculture as an engineer might conceive it to be. Nature has introduced great variety into the landscape, but man has displayed a passion for simplifying it. Thus he undoes the built-in checks and balances by which nature holds the species within bounds. One important natural check is a limit on the amount of suitable habitat for each species. Obviously then, an insect that lives on wheat can build up its population to much higher levels on a farm devoted to wheat than on one in which wheat is intermingled with other crops to which the insect is not adapted.

The same thing happens in other situations. A generation or more ago, the towns of large areas of the United States lined their streets with the noble elm tree. Now the beauty they hopefully created is threatened with complete destruction as disease sweeps through the elms, carried by a beetle that would have only limited chance to build up large populations and to spread from tree to tree if the elms were only occasional trees in a richly diversified planting.

Another factor in the modern insect problem is one that must be viewed against a background of geologic and human history: the spreading of thousands of different kinds of organisms from their native homes to invade new territories. This worldwide migration has been studied and graphically described by the British ecologist Charles Elton in his recent book *The Ecology of Invasions.* During the Cretaceous Period, some hundred million years ago, flooding seas cut many land bridges between continents and living things found themselves confined in what Elton calls "colossal separate nature reserves." There, isolated from others of their kind, they developed many new species. When some of the land masses were joined again, about 15 million years ago, these species began to move out into new territories—a movement that is not only still in progress but is now receiving considerable assistance from man.

The importation of plants is the primary agent in the modern spread of species, for animals have almost invariably gone along with the plants, quarantine being a comparatively recent and not completely effective innovation. The United States Office of Plant Introduction alone has introduced almost 200,000 species and varieties of plants from all over the world. Nearly half of the 180 or so major insect enemies of plants in the United States are accidental imports from abroad, and most of them have come as hitchhikers on plants.

In new territory, out of reach of the restraining hand of the natural enemies that kept down its numbers in its native land, an invading plant or animal is able to become enormously abundant. Thus it is no accident that our most troublesome insects are introduced species.

These invasions, both the naturally occurring and those dependent on human assistance, are likely to continue indefinitely. Quarantine and massive chemical campaigns are only extremely expensive ways of buying time. We are faced, according to Dr. Elton, "with a life-and-death need not just to find new technological means of suppressing this plant or that animal"; instead we need the basic knowledge of animal populations and their relations to their surroundings that will "promote an even balance and damp down the explosive power of outbreaks and new invasions."

Much of the necessary knowledge is now available but we do not use it. We train ecologists in our universities and even employ them in our governmental agencies but we seldom take their advice. We allow the chemical death rain to fall as though there were no alternative, whereas in fact there are many, and our ingenuity could soon discover many more if given opportunity.

Have we fallen into a mesmerized state that makes us accept as inevitable that which is inferior or detrimental, as though having lost the will or the vision to demand that which is good? Such thinking, in the words of the ecologist Paul Shepard, "idealizes life with only its head out of water, inches above the limits of toleration of the corruption of its own environment . . . Why should we tolerate a diet of weak poisons, a home in insipid surroundings, a circle of acquaintances who are not quite our enemies, the noise of motors with just enough relief to prevent insanity? Who would want to live in a world which is just not quite fatal?"

Yet such a world is pressed upon us. The crusade to create a chemically sterile, insect-free world seems to have engendered a fanatic zeal on the part of many specialists and most of the so-called control agencies. On every hand there is evidence that those engaged in spraying operations exercise a ruthless power. "The regulatory entomologists . . . function as prosecutor, judge and jury, tax assessor and collector and sheriff to enforce their own orders," said Connecticut entomologist Neely Turner. The most flagrant abuses go unchecked in both state and federal agencies.

It is not my contention that chemical insecticides must never be used. I do contend that we have put poisonous and biologically potent chemicals indiscriminately into the hands of persons largely or wholly ignorant of their potentials for harm. We have subjected enormous numbers of people to contact with these poisons, without their consent and often without their knowledge. If the Bill of Rights contains no guarantee that a citizen shall be secure against lethal poisons distributed either by private individuals or by public officials, it is surely only because our forefathers, despite their considerable wisdom and foresight, could conceive of no such problem.

I contend, furthermore, that we have allowed these chemicals to be used with little or no advance investigation of their effect on soil, water, wildlife, and man himself. Future generations are unlikely to condone our lack of prudent concern for the integrity of the natural world that supports all life.

There is still very limited awareness of the nature of the threat. This is an era of specialists, each of whom sees his own problem and is unaware of or intolerant of the larger frame into which it fits. It is also an era dominated by industry, in which the right to make a dollar at whatever cost is seldom challenged. When the public protests, confronted with some obvious evidence of damaging results of pesticide applications, it is fed little tranquilizing pills of half truth. We urgently need an end to these false assurances, to the sugar coating of unpalatable facts. It is the public that is being asked to assume the risks that the insect controllers calculate. The public must decide whether it wishes to continue on the present road, and it can do so only when in full possession of the facts. In the words of Jean Rostand, "The obligation to endure gives us the right to know."

Questions on Meaning

1. How has the nature of pollution changed in the twentieth century that so concerns Carson? What examples does she give of this new pollution?
2. How many new chemicals are introduced each year (the 1960s) according to Carson? How many herbicides and pesticides had been introduced in the preceding 15–20 years? What does Carson mean by "nonselective chemicals"?
3. Describe the "process of escalation" of pesticide use. How does this "vindicate" Darwin? When and how would Carson agree to the use of chemical insecticides?

Questions on Rhetorical Strategy and Style

1. Examine how Carson uses a cause and effect writing strategy in her description of how the earth's environment impacts the vegetation and animal life it supports. How did this relationship change in the twentieth century? What is the role of time in the relationship between the earth's environment and life on earth; how has the pace of change been altered?
2. What does Carson's use of such wording as "chain of evil" and "sinister" say about her point of view? What impact do these strong, opinionated terms have on her argument?
3. Note how Carson analyzes the process of organism invasion. How have people accelerated that process? Why does an invading organism often grow or reproduce in great numbers in new territory?

Writing Assignments

1. Carson's writing helped spur the organic farming movement. What is an accurate definition of organic farming? What are the supposed benefits of organically raised animals and organically grown crops? What is the trend today toward organic farming, both in terms of product sales and acres farmed?
2. If Carson objected to "man's tampering with the atom," which has resulted with radiation entering the environment via nuclear weapons, nuclear energy, and other nuclear activities, how do you believe she would respond to today's genetic engineering? Research the ethics of genetic engineering. What are some of the objections raised by opponents?

3. The pesticide malathion has been used fairly widely in recent years in attempts to control fruit flies and mosquitoes. Proponents claim it is safe and effective; opponents argue that no chemical spray is safe and that malathion is *in*effective. Research the debate over malathion and write an essay arguing one position or the other. If you live in an area where malathion is used, interview a health department official for additional insight. Cite scientific evidence of its safety or harm and reports of its efficacy. If you oppose malathion, what would you suggest as an alternative?

I'm a Banana and Proud of It

Wayson Choy

Wayson Choy (1939–) was born in Vancouver and now lives in Toronto, where he teaches at Humber College. His first novel, The Jade Peony *(1995), was awarded the Trillium Award for best book of 1996, an award he shared with Margaret Atwood. He has also published* Paper Shadows: A Chinatown Childhood *(2001), a book about growing up in Vancouver's Chinatown, and is currently at work on* The Ten Thousand Things, *a sequel to* The Jade Peony. *In the following essay, which first appeared in* The Globe and Mail, *Choy considers the significance of nicknames and their ability to appropriately reflect those who have them assigned to them.*

1 Because both my parents came from China, I took Chinese. But 1
I cannot read or write Chinese and barely speak it. I love my North American citizenship. I don't mind being called a "banana," yellow on the outside and white inside. I'm proud I'm a banana.

After all, in Canada and the United States, native Indians are "apples" (red outside, white inside); blacks are "Oreo cookies" (black and white); and Chinese are "bananas." These metaphors assume, both rightly and wrongly, that the culture here has been primarily anglo-white. Cultural history made me a banana.

History: My father and mother arrived separately to the B.C. coast in the early part of the century. They came as unwanted "aliens." Better to be an alien here than to be dead of starvation in China. But after the Chinese Exclusion laws were passed in North America (late 1800s,

"I'm a Banana and Proud of It," by Wayson Choy from *The Globe and Mail.* Reprinted by permission of the author.

early 1900s), no Chinese immigrants were granted citizenship in either Canada or the United States.

Like those Old China village men from *Toi San* who, in the 1850s, laid down cliff-edge train tracks through the Rockies and the Sierras, or like those first women who came as mail-order wives or concubines and who as bond-slaves were turned into cheaper labourers or even prostitutes—like many of those men and women, my father and mother survived ugly, unjust times. In 1917, two hours after he got off the boat from Hong Kong, my father was called "chink" and told to go back to China. "Chink" is a hateful racist term, stereotyping the shape of Asian eyes: "a chink in the armour," an undesirable slit. For the Elders, the past was humiliating. Eventually, the Second World War changed hostile attitudes toward the Chinese.

During the war, Chinese men volunteered and lost their lives as members of the American and Canadian military. When hostilities ended, many more were proudly in uniform waiting to go overseas. Record Chinatown dollars were raised to buy War Bonds. After 1945, challenged by such money and ultimate sacrifices, the Exclusion laws in both Canada and the United States were revoked. Chinatown residents claimed their citizenship and sent for their families.

By 1949, after the Communists took over China, those of us who arrived here as young children, or were born here, stayed. No longer "aliens," we became legal citizens of North America. Many of us also became "bananas."

Historically, "banana" is not a racist term. Although it clumsily stereotypes many of the children and grandchildren of the Old Chinatowns, the term actually follows the old Chinese tendency to assign endearing nicknames to replace formal names, semicomic names to keep one humble. Thus, "banana" describes the generations who assimilated so well into North American life.

In fact, our families encouraged members of my generation in the 1950s and sixties to "get ahead," to get an English education, to get a job with good pay and prestige. "Don't work like me," Chinatown parents said. "Work in an office!" The *lao wahkiu* (the Chinatown old-timers) also warned, "Never forget—you still be Chinese!"

None of us ever forgot. The mirror never lied.

Many Chinatown teen-agers felt we didn't quite belong in any one world. We looked Chinese, but thought and behaved North American.

Impatient Chinatown parents wanted the best of both worlds for us, but they bluntly labelled their children and grandchildren "*juk-sing*" or even "*mo no*." Not that we were totally "shallow bamboo butt-ends" or entirely "no brain," but we had less and less understanding of Old China traditions, and less and less interest in their village histories. Father used to say we lacked Taoist ritual, Taoist manners. We were, he said, "*mo li*."

This was true. Chinatown's younger brains, like everyone else's of whatever race, were being colonized by "white bread" U.S. family television programs. We began to feel Chinese home life was inferior. We co-operated with English-language magazines that showed us how to act and what to buy. Seductive Hollywood movies made some of us secretly weep that we did not have moviestar faces. American music made Chinese music sound like noise.

By the 1970s and eighties, many of us had consciously or unconsciously distanced ourselves from our Chinatown histories. We became bananas.

Finally, for me, in my 40s or 50s, with the death first of my mother, then my father, I realized I did not belong anywhere unless I could understand the past. I needed to find the foundation of my Chinese-ness. I needed roots.

I spent my college holidays researching the past. I read Chinatown oral histories, located documents, searched out early articles. Those early citizens came back to life for me. Their long toil and blood sacrifices, the proud record of their patient, legal challenges, gave us all our present rights as citizens. Canadian and American Chinatowns set aside their family tongue differences and encouraged each other to fight injustice. There were no borders. "After all," they affirmed, "*Daaih ga tohng yahn* . . . We are all Chinese!"

15 In my book, *The Jade Peony,* I tried to recreate this past, to explore 15
the beginnings of the conflicts trapped within myself, the struggle between being Chinese and being North American. I discovered a truth: these "between world" struggles are universal.

In every human being, there is "the Other"—something that makes each of us feel how different we are to everyone else, even to family members. Yet, ironically, we are all the same, wanting the same security and happiness. I know this now.

I think the early Chinese pioneers actually started "going bananas" from the moment they first settled upon the West Coast. They had no choice. They adapted. They initiated assimilation. If they had not, they and their family would have starved to death. I might even suggest that all surviving Chinatown citizens eventually became bananas. Only some, of course, were more ripe than others.

That's why I'm proudly a banana: I accept the paradox of being both Chinese and not Chinese.

Now at last, whenever I look in the mirror or hear ghost voices shouting, "You still Chinese!," I smile.

I know another truth: In immigrant North America, we are all Chinese.

Questions on Meaning

1. Choy distinguishes between nicknames and racist terms. Why does Choy consider "banana" not racist? Why might someone find the term offensive? How would you explain the difference between these two categories?
2. Many immigrants have written about the challenges of maintaining one's cultural heritage while simultaneously seeking assimilation. Why is this situation, in Choy's word, paradoxical?
3. What are some of the other ways in which different social groups characterize themselves in an effort to maintain their ethnic and racial identities?

Questions on Strategy and Style

1. How would you characterize Choy's voice in this essay? Is it appealing to you? If so, why? What kind of person do you take him to be?
2. In his essay Choy often uses the term "banana." What effect does the term take on as it is repeated throughout? Do you think the author had a specific reason for using the term as often as he did?
3. Why did Choy write this essay? Who are his intended readers and what is he trying to accomplish with them? Why might the essay be important to his primary readers?

Writing Assignments

1. The use of nicknames, particularly during childhood, is common in our society. Write a memory piece in which you recall different people from your past and the names people gave them, or they gave themselves. Describe how those people received those names or came to use them. Discuss how those names reflected or characterized them. What function do you imagine the names had for these people?
2. The Choy essay is about cultural or ethnic heritage. As we know, most people in North America have a heritage that began in another country. Genealogy has become a popular hobby. Perhaps the trend reflects developments in our society. There are numerous genealogical sites on the Internet. Go to one of them and produce your own family history. Write it up as a narrative.

Why I Want a Wife

Judy Brady

Judy Brady (1937–), born in San Francisco, studied painting and received a B.F.A. in 1962 in art from the University of Iowa. Then she married and raised a family in a traditional housewife role. She later commented that her male professors had talked her out of pursuing a career in education. In the late 1960s, she became active in the women's movement and began writing articles on feminism and other social issues. In 1990, she was the editor of Women and Cancer, *an anthology by women. The essay "Why I Want a Wife" appeared in the first issue of* Ms. *magazine in 1972.*

1 I belong to that classification of people known as wives. I am A 1
Wife. And, not altogether incidentally, I am a mother.

Not too long ago a male friend of mine appeared on the scene fresh from a recent divorce. He had one child, who is, of course, with his ex-wife. He is looking for another wife. As I thought about him while I was ironing one evening, it suddenly occurred to me that I, too, would like to have a wife. Why do I want a wife?

I would like to go back to school so that I can become economically independent, support myself, and, if need be, support those dependent upon me. I want a wife who will work and send me to school. And while I am going to school I want a wife to take care of my children. I want a wife to keep track of the children's doctor and dentist appointments. And to keep track of mine, too. I want a wife to make sure my children eat properly and are kept clean. I want a wife who will wash the children's clothes and keep them mended. I want a wife who is a good nurturant attendant to my children, who arranges for their schooling, makes sure that they have an adequate social life with their peers, takes them to the park, the zoo, etc. I want a wife who takes care of the children when they are sick, a wife who arranges to be around when the children need special care, because, of course, I cannot miss classes at school. My wife must arrange to lose time at work and not lose the job. It may mean a small cut in my wife's income from time to time, but I guess I can tolerate that. Needless to say, my wife will arrange and pay for the care of the children while my wife is working.

I want a wife who will take care of *my* physical needs. I want a wife who will keep my house clean, a wife who will pick up after me. I want a wife who will keep my clothes clean, ironed, mended, replaced when need be, and who will see to it that my personal things are kept in their proper place so that I can find what I need the minute I need it. I want a wife who cooks the meals, a wife who is a *good* cook. I want a wife who will plan the menus, do the necessary grocery shopping, prepare the meals, serve them pleasantly, and then do the cleaning up while I do my studying. I want a wife who will care for me when I am sick and sympathize with my pain and loss of time from school. I want a wife to go along when our family takes a vacation so that someone can continue to care for me and my children when I need a rest and change of scene.

5 I want a wife who will not bother me with rambling complaints 5
about a wife's duties. But I want a wife who will listen to me when I feel the need to explain a rather difficult point I have come across in my course of studies. And I want a wife who will type my papers for me when I have written them.

I want a wife who will take care of the details of my social life. When my wife and I are invited out by friends, I want a wife who will take care of the babysitting arrangements. When I meet people at school that I like and want to entertain, I want a wife who will have the house clean, will prepare a special meal, serve it to me and my friends, and not interrupt when I talk about the things that interest me and my friends. I want a wife who will have arranged that the children are fed and ready for bed before my guests arrive so that the children do not bother us. I want a wife who takes care of the needs of my guests so that they feel comfortable, who makes sure that they have an ashtray, that they are passed the hors d'oeuvres, that they are offered a second helping of the food, that their wine glasses are replenished when necessary, that their coffee is served to them as they like it. And I want a wife who knows that sometimes I need a night out by myself.

I want a wife who is sensitive to my sexual needs, a wife who makes love passionately and eagerly when I feel like it, a wife who makes sure that I am satisfied. And, of course, I want a wife who will not demand sexual attention when I am not in the mood for it. I want a wife who assumes the complete responsibility for birth control, because I do not want more children. I want a wife who will remain sexually faithful to me so that I do not have to clutter up my intellectual life with jealousies. And I want a wife who understands that *my* sexual needs may entail more than strict adherence to monogamy. I must, after all, be able to relate to people as fully as possible.

If, by chance, I find another person more suitable as a wife than the wife I already have, I want the liberty to replace my present wife with another one. Naturally, I will expect a fresh, new life; my wife will take the children and be solely responsible for them so that I am left free.

When I am through with school and have a job, I want my wife to quit working and remain at home so that my wife can more fully and completely take care of a wife's duties.

10 My God, who *wouldn't* want a wife? 10

Key Terms

nurturant
tolerate
sympathetic
rambling
interrupt
hors d'oeuvres
replenished
adherence
monogamy

Questions on Meaning

1. What kind of wife does Brady want? What would this wife do for her? What characteristics would the wife have?
2. What is your reaction to this essay? Do you think that it is funny, or is it offensive? Are you confused by the gender of the writer?
3. What is Brady saying about the attitudes of men toward their wives? The essay was written over thirty years ago. How have things changed? How have things not changed?

Questions on Rhetorical Strategy and Style

1. This essay is sarcastic from the first line to the last. How does the sarcasm affect the reader of the essay?
2. The essay uses the first person over and over again, repeatedly using *I* and *me.* Why does Brady uses the first person so much?
3. The essay ends with a question. What effect does this question have? How does the ending make the point of the essay clear? Are there still people who marry other people for their usefulness?

Writing Assignments

1. Consider a role that you have experience with in your life. Then write an essay about how you would like to have the perfect teacher, mother, waiter, or some such person who is expected to

help others. What do you discover about your expectations as you write this essay?

2. Interview a few people you know who were married thirty years ago. Ask them about what they expected in a spouse and how the reality of their marriage compares to their original expectations. Write an essay about the responses.
3. What causes people to marry in the twenty-first century? Evaluate the reasons why people get married and write an essay. You may want to do some kind of satire such as Brady's or you may want to write seriously.

I Have a Dream

Martin Luther King, Jr.

Martin Luther King, Jr. (1929–1968) was born in Atlanta, Georgia, the son and grandson of Baptist ministers. His college and postgraduate studies took him from Moorhouse College to Crozer Theological Seminary to Boston University, where he received a Ph.D. (1955) and met his future wife, Coretta Scott. King's active involvement in the civil rights movement began in 1955, when he led a boycott of segregated buses in Montgomery, Alabama. From the mid-1950s until he was shot and killed in Memphis, Tennessee, while supporting striking city workers, King organized boycotts, sit-ins, mass demonstrations, and other protest activities. As a black civil rights leader, King was arrested, jailed, stoned, stabbed, and beaten; his house was bombed; and he was placed under secret surveillance by Federal Bureau of Investigation (FBI) director J. Edgar Hoover. Through his leadership—always underscored by his nonviolent beliefs—King's name has become synonymous with the watersheds of the civil rights movement in the United States: Rosa Parks, the Southern Christian Leadership Conference, Selma, Alabama, the Civil Rights Act, and the Voting Rights Act. His crowning moment occurred during the August 1963 civil rights march on Washington, D.C., when King, standing in front of the Lincoln Memorial, delivered his most famous speech, this essay. A year later he would receive the Nobel Peace Prize. As you read King's words, spoken nearly a century after Lincoln signed the Emancipation Proclamation, listen to this great orator; try to feel the emotion that hundreds of thousands of black Americans carried to the Esplanade that memorable day.

---

1 I am happy to join with you today in what will go down in history as the greatest demonstration for freedom in the history of our nation.

Five score years ago, a great American, in whose symbolic shadow we stand today, signed the Emancipation Proclamation. This momentous decree came as a great beacon light of hope to millions of Negro slaves who had been seared in the flames of withering injustice. It came as a joyous daybreak to end the long night of their captivity. But one hundred years later, the Negro is still not free. One hundred years later, the life of the Negro is still sadly crippled by the manacles of segregation and the chains of discrimination. One hundred years later, the Negro lives on a lonely island of poverty in the midst of a vast ocean of material prosperity. One hundred years later, the Negro is still anguished in the corners of American society and finds himself in exile in his own land. And so we have come here today to dramatize a shameful condition.

In a sense we have come to our nation's capital to cash a check. When the architects of our republic wrote the magnificent words of the Constitution and the Declaration of Independence, they were signing a promissory note to which every American was to fall heir. This note was the promise that all men—yes, Black men as well as white men—would be guaranteed the inalienable rights of life, liberty, and the pursuit of happiness.

It is obvious today that America has defaulted on this promissory note insofar as her citizens of color are concerned. Instead of honoring this sacred obligation, America has given the Negro people a bad check, a check which has come back marked "insufficient funds." But we refuse to believe that the bank of justice is bankrupt. We refuse to believe that there are insufficient funds in the great vaults of opportunity of this nation; and so we have come to cash this check, a check that will give us upon demand the riches of freedom and the security of justice.

5 We have also come to this hallowed spot to remind America of the fierce urgency of *now.* This is no time to engage in the luxury of cooling off or to take the tranquilizing drug of gradualism. Now is the time to make real the promises of democracy. Now is the time to rise from the dark and desolate valley of segregation to the sunlit patch of racial justice. Now is the time to lift our nation from the quicksands of racial injustice to the solid rock of brotherhood. Now is the time to make justice a reality for all of God's children.

It would be fatal for the nation to overlook the urgency of the moment. This sweltering summer of the Negro's legitimate discontent will not pass until there is an invigorating autumn of freedom and equality. Nineteen Sixty-three is not an end, but a beginning. And those who hope that the Negro needed to blow off steam and will now be content will have a rude awakening if the nation returns to business as usual. There will be neither rest nor tranquility in America until the Negro is granted his citizenship rights. The whirlwinds of revolt will continue to shake the foundations of our nation until the bright day of justice emerges.

But there is something that I must say to my people who stand on the warm threshold which leads into the palace of justice. In the process of gaining our rightful place, we must not be guilty of wrongful deeds. Let us not seek to satisfy our thirst for freedom by drinking from the cup of bitterness and hatred. We must forever conduct our struggle on the high plane of dignity and discipline. We must not allow our creative protest to degenerate into physical violence. Again and again we must rise to the majestic heights of meeting physical force with soul force. And the marvelous new militancy which has engulfed the Negro community must not lead us to a distrust of all white people; for many of our white brothers, as evidenced by their presence here today, have come to realize that their destiny is tied up with our destiny, and they have come to realize that their freedom is inextricably bound to our freedom.

We cannot walk alone. And as we walk we must make the pledge that we shall always march ahead. We cannot turn back. There are those who are asking the devotees of civil rights, "When will you be satisfied?" We can never be satisfied as long as the Negro is the victim of the unspeakable horrors of police brutality. We can never be satisfied as long as our bodies, heavy with the fatigue of travel, cannot gain lodging in the motels of the highways and the hotels of the cities. We cannot be satisfied as long as the Negro's basic mobility is from a smaller ghetto to a larger one. We can never be satisfied as long as our children are stripped of their selfhood and robbed of their dignity by signs stating "For Whites Only." We cannot be satisfied as long as the Negro in Mississippi cannot vote and a Negro in New York believes he has nothing for which to vote. No, no, we are not satisfied, and we will not be satisfied until justice rolls down like waters and righteousness like a mighty stream.

I am not unmindful that some of you have come here out of great trials and tribulations. Some of you have come fresh from narrow jail cells. Some of you have come from areas where your quest for freedom left you battered by the storms of persecution and staggered by the winds of police brutality. You have been the veterans of creative suffering. Continue to work with the faith that unearned suffering is redemptive.

Go back to Mississippi, and go back to Alabama. Go back to South Carolina. Go back to Georgia. Go back to Louisiana. Go back to the slums and ghettos of our Northern cities, knowing that somehow this situation can and will be changed. Let us not wallow in the valley of despair.

I say to you today, my friends, even though we face the difficulties of today and tomorrow, I still have a dream. It is a dream deeply rooted in the American dream. I have a dream that one day this nation will rise up and live out the true meaning of its creed: "We hold these truths to be self-evident, that all men are created equal." I have a dream that one day, on the red hills of Georgia, sons of former slaves and the sons of former slave owners will be able to sit down together at the table of brotherhood. I have a dream that one day even the state of Mississippi, a state sweltering with the heat of injustice, sweltering with the heat of oppression, will be transformed into an oasis of freedom and justice. I have a dream that my four little children will one day live in a nation where they will not be judged by the color of their skin, but by the content of their character.

I have a dream today. I have a dream that one day down in Alabama—with its vicious racists, with its governor's lips dripping with the words of interposition and nullification—one day right there in Alabama, little Black boys and Black girls will be able to join hands with little white boys and white girls as sisters and brothers.

I have a dream today. I have a dream that one day every valley shall be exalted and every hill and mountain shall be made low, the rough places will be made plain and the crooked places will be made straight, and the glory of the Lord shall be revealed, and all flesh shall see it together.

This is our hope. This is the faith that I go back to the South with. And with this faith we will be able to hew out of the mountain of despair a stone of hope. With this faith we will be able to transform the jangling discords of our nation into a beautiful symphony of brotherhood. With this faith we will be able to work together, to play together, to struggle together, to go to jail together, to stand up for freedom together, knowing that we will be free one day.

And this will be the day—this will be the day when all of God's children will be able to sing with new meaning.

My country, 'tis of thee,
Sweet land of liberty,
Of thee I sing;
Land where my fathers died,
Land of the Pilgrims' pride,
From every mountainside
Let freedom ring.

And if America is to be a great nation, this must become true.

And so let freedom ring from the prodigious hilltops of New Hampshire. Let freedom ring from the mighty mountains of New York. Let freedom ring from the heightening Alleghenies of Pennsylvania. Let freedom ring from the snow-capped Rockies of Colorado. Let freedom ring from the curvaceous slopes of California.

But not only that. Let freedom ring from Stone Mountain of Georgia. Let freedom ring from Lookout Mountain of Tennessee. Let freedom ring from every hill and molehill of Mississippi. "From every mountainside let freedom ring."

And when this happens—when we allow freedom to ring, when we let it ring from every village and every hamlet, from every state and every city—we will be able to speed up that day when all of God's children, Black men and white men, Jews and Gentiles, Protestants and Catholics, will be able to join hands and sing in the words of the old Negro spiritual: "Free at last! Free at last! Thank God Almighty. We are free at last!"

Key Terms

momentous
withering
manacles
promissory
inalienable
gradualism
interposition
nullification

Questions on Meaning

1. In this famous 1963 speech King tells his listeners that African Americans have not yet been freed, despite the fact that the Emancipation Proclamation legally freed them one hundred years before. How does he show that they are not yet free?
2. While the threat of violence in society over the issue of race was a strong presence in the 1960s, King tells his followers to avoid violent actions. He also asks his followers not to distrust all white people. Why does he have to ask for these things?
3. In the speech, King addresses African Americans who have gathered before him from all over the nation. He instructs them to return to their states and work for freedom and their right to succeed at the American dream. How does he make this plea personal to his listeners?

Questions on Rhetorical Strategy and Style

1. This speech is widely regarded as a masterpiece and is best understood by viewing it on film. Why does King begin with five score years ago, five times twenty, rather than with one hundred years ago? What speech is he asking his listeners to remember?
2. King was a preacher. Word choices such as "Go back to Mississippi, and go back to Alabama," echo the great spiritual, "Go Down Moses." Find other places in the speech where King uses biblical references or references to spirituals and hymns.

3. This speech follows the pattern of growing enthusiasm that characterizes many famous speeches. How does the ending show the energy and force of that enthusiasm?

Writing Assignments

1. The south has changed radically since King gave this speech. Many African Americans are moving from the north to the south because of better living conditions and increased opportunities. How has your own community changed for minority groups? Write an essay describing the current state of conditions for minorities in your home town.
2. Find a source of injustice or unfairness that moves you. Write a speech that asks for the righting of that injustice. Work to use your own authority on the subject, using either your knowledge or your involvement in the situation, or both.
3. Write about your own response to this speech as a person living in the twenty-first century.

Back to Nature

Gary Snyder

Gary Snyder was born in 1930 in San Francisco. A poet, essayist, and environmentalist, his writing is heavily influenced by the Zen Buddhist training he received in Japan. He is also associated with Beat Movement figures such as Jack Kerouac and Allen Ginsberg. He has worked as a seaman, a logger, and a forest lookout for the Forest Service. A few of his most recent titles include No Nature *(1992) and* The Practice of the Wild *(1990). In 1974, he was awarded the Pulitzer Prize for poetry for* Turtle Island. *In the following selection, Snyder reveals why some might label him a modern day Thoreau by offering his plan for how we might yet return to nature.*

1 If societies were incapable of surprising shifts and turns, if religions 1
and philosophies, languages, and clothing never changed, we'd surely have to grimly crunch away in the same old story and eventually drown in some sort of *Blade Runner*-type movie. Walter Truett Anderson ("There's no Going Back to Nature," September/October) seems to assume that the track we're on will go forever and nobody will learn much. He provides some excellent information, he is clearly sincere, but it's basically the same old engineering, business, and bureaucracy message with its lank rhetoric of data and management.

The oh-so-foolish deep ecologists, greens, ecofeminists, etc., are out there—at almost no cost to the system—providing imagination, vision, passion, a deeply felt ethical stance, and in many cases some living examples of practice. The ethical position that would accord intrinsic value to non-human nature, and would see human beings as

"Back to Nature," by Gary Synder, reprinted from *Mother Jones,* Sept/Oct 1996. Reprinted with permission by the author.

involved in moral as well as practical choices in regard to the natural world, makes all the difference.

I have no quarrel with restoring creeks, crunching understory fuel load, logging out genuinely sick trees, hanging out counting the frogs in the creek, taping owl calls, piling up data in the workstation, and all that. I do it myself. It it's done with the commodity mind, you might as well be managing a concentration camp. If it's done with the mind of the natural neighborhood, with the intimacy that comes with knowing yourself as a member of the ecosystem, then those very same chores are a matter of working with and learning from the non-human critters in the 'hood. It becomes a collaboration, a feast, a memorial gathering, a ceremony. This is what deep ecology is about. The ethic of concern for all beings including the non-human, incidentally, is not just some invention of New Agers, Norwegian philosophers, or Native American academicians, but is anciently and deeply rooted worldwide, going back for millennia. Buddhism and much of Hinduism put this ethic at the top of their list of precepts.

I think it's clear, in this election campaign year, we can't afford to trash any values. They'll all come in handy.

5 Mr. Anderson quotes me correctly—from a mid-'80s issue of *Sierra* magazine where I spoke on bioregions and place. And indeed I do believe that more people staying put, learning their place, and taking on some active role, would improve our social and ecological life. I said people should try to become "*paysans, paisano, peones*," meaning people of the land, people of the place. But note: I didn't specify how big the place can be. The size of place one becomes a member of is limited only by the size of one's heart. We speak of watershed consciousness, and the great water cycle of the planet makes it all one watershed. We are all natives to this earth. Yet one has to start where one is and become nature-literate to the scale of the immediate home place. With home-based knowledge, it is then within our power to get a glimpse of the planet as home. As a rule though, local knowledge (combined with an understanding of the dynamics of systems) remains the most useful, and the most delicious.

No one ever said that "don't move" means you can't go on trips—peasants of Japan, religious devotees of India have always gone on long pilgrimages to the mountains after harvest was over. The thing is, even when on a trip, you are always clear as to where you came from. We can be thankful that bioregional practice is more sophisticated than some replay of the medieval village. Since it is a line of thought for the future, it calls us to be ecologically and culturally cosmopolitan, hip to the plant and weather zones of the whole world, as well as to the cuisine and architecture.

As for technology: Smarter bombs, faster computers, and quieter chainsaws certainly have their place. The struggle for the integrity of the environment will need good tools—the good guys want their computers to be as big and fast as those of the bad guys. Understandably. But though weapons win battles, they don't win the peace. Peace is won by winning hearts and minds. Watershed imagining, bioregional ideas of governance, the actual existence of communities that include the non-human in their embrace, myths of ecological justice, the thought of enlightenment—all this nutty ancient stuff is a matter of engaging hearts and minds.

Questions on Meaning

1. According to Snyder, what should be our relationship to nature? What does he mean by the "ethic of concern for all beings, including non-human"?
2. How does Snyder use the term "ecosystem"? What does he mean by "deep ecology"?

Questions on Rhetorical Strategy and Style

1. How would you describe the tone of this essay? What does this suggest about the author's attitude toward his audience?
2. What reasons does Snyder give to support his idea about deep ecology? What makes his argument persuasive?

Writing Assignments

1. Are the interests of the environment and business incompatible? Write an opinion paper defending or contradicting this position.
2. Write a narrative essay about one of your "back to nature" experiences. Let it answer the question of whether going back to nature is possible in these times.

The Jacket

Gary Soto

Gary Soto (1952–) was born in Fresno, California. In addition to teaching at the University of California at Berkeley, Soto has written poetry, memoirs, essays, and children's fiction. His books, which often reflect his Mexican-American roots, include the poetry collections The Elements of San Joaquin *(1977) and* Black Hair *(1985) and the memoirs* Living Up the Street *(1985),* Small Faces *(1986),* Lesser Evils *(1988), and* A Summer Life *(1990). Soto describes the sometimes overwhelming significance of clothing to adolescents in this essay from* Small Faces.

1 My clothes have failed me. I remember the green coat that I 1
wore in fifth and sixth grade when you either danced like a champ or pressed yourself against a greasy wall, bitter as a penny toward the happy couples.

When I needed a new jacket and my mother asked what kind I wanted, I described something like bikers wear: black leather and silver studs, with enough belts to hold down a small town. We were in the kitchen, steam on the windows from her cooking. She listened so long while stirring dinner that I thought she understood for sure the kind I wanted. The next day when I got home from school, I discovered draped on my bedpost a jacket the color of day-old guacamole. I threw my books on the bed and approached the jacket slowly, as if it were a stranger whose hand I had to shake. I touched the vinyl sleeve, the collar, and peeked at the mustard-colored lining.

From the kitchen mother yelled that my jacket was in the closet. I closed the door to her voice and pulled at the rack of clothes in the closet, hoping the jacket on the bedpost wasn't for me but my mean brother. No luck. I gave up. From my bed, I stared at the jacket. I wanted to cry because it was so ugly and so big that I knew I'd have to wear it a long time. I was a small kid, thin as a young tree, and it would be years before I'd have a new one. I stared at the jacket, like an enemy, thinking bad things before I took off my old jacket, whose sleeves climbed halfway to my elbow.

I put the big jacket on. I zipped it up and down several times and rolled the cuffs up so they didn't cover my hands. I put my hands in the pockets and flapped the jacket like a bird's wings. I stood in front of the mirror, full face, then profile, and then looked over my shoulder as if someone had called me. I sat on the bed, stood against the bed, and combed my hair to see what I would look like doing something natural. I looked ugly. I threw it on my brother's bed and looked at it for a long time before I slipped it on and went out to the backyard, smiling a "thank you" to my mom as I passed her in the kitchen. With my hands in my pockets I kicked a ball against the fence, and then climbed it to sit looking into the alley. I hurled orange peels at the mouth of an open garbage can, and when the peels were gone I watched the white puffs of my breath thin to nothing.

5 I jumped down, hands in my pockets, and in the backyard, on my 5
knees, I teased my dog, Brownie, by swooping my arms while making bird calls. He jumped at me and missed. He jumped again and again, until a tooth sunk deep, ripping an L-shaped tear on my left sleeve. I pushed Brownie away to study the tear as I would a cut on my arm. There was no blood, only a few loose pieces of fuzz. Damn dog, I thought, and pushed him away hard when he tried to bite again. I got up from my knees and went to my bedroom to sit with my jacket on my lap, with the lights out.

That was the first afternoon with my new jacket. The next day I wore it to sixth grade and got a D on a math quiz. During the morning recess Frankie T., the playground terrorist, pushed me to the ground and told me to stay there until recess was over. My best friend, Steve Negrete, ate an apple while looking at me, and the girls turned away to whisper on the monkey bars. The teachers were no help: they looked my way and talked about how foolish I looked in my new jacket. I saw their heads bob with laughter, their hands half covering their mouths.

Even though it was cold, I took off the jacket during lunch and played kickball in a thin shirt, my arms feeling like braille from goose bumps. But when I returned to class I slipped the jacket on and shivered until I was warm. I sat on my hands, heating them up, while my

teeth chattered like a cup of crooked dice. Finally warm, I slid out of the jacket but put it back on a few minutes later when the fire bell rang. We paraded out into the yard where we, the sixth graders, walked past all the other grades to stand against the back fence. Everybody saw me. Although they didn't say out loud, "Man, that's ugly," I heard the buzz-buzz of gossip and even laughter that I knew was meant for me.

And so I went, in my guacamole-colored jacket. So embarrassed, so hurt, I couldn't even do my homework. I received C's on quizzes and forgot the state capitals and the rivers of South America, our friendly neighbor. Even the girls who had been friendly blew away like loose flowers to follow the boys in neat jackets.

I wore that thing for three years until the sleeves grew short and my forearms stuck out like the necks of turtles. All during that time no love came to me—no little dark girl in a Sunday dress she wore on Monday. At lunchtime I stayed with the ugly boys who leaned against the chainlink fence and looked around with propellers of grass spinning in our mouths. We saw girls walk by alone, saw couples, hand in hand, their heads like bookends pressing air together. We saw them and spun our propellers so fast our faces were blurs.

10 I blame that jacket for those bad years. I blame my mother for her 10
bad taste and her cheap ways. It was a sad time for the heart. With a friend I spent my sixth-grade year in a tree in the alley, waiting for something good to happen to me in that jacket, which had become the ugly brother who tagged along wherever I went. And it was about that time that I began to grow. My chest puffed up with muscle and, strangely, a few more ribs. Even my hands, those fleshy hammers, showed bravely through the cuffs, the fingers already hardening for the coming fights. But that L-shaped rip on the left sleeve got bigger; bits of stuffing coughed out from its wound after a hard day of play. I finally Scotch-taped it closed, but in rain or cold weather the tape peeled off like a scab and more stuffing fell out until that sleeve shriveled into a palsied arm. That winter the elbows began to crack and whole chunks of green began to fall off. I showed the cracks to my mother, who always seemed to be at the stove with steamed-up glasses, and she said that there were children in Mexico who would love that jacket. I told her that this was America and yelled that Debbie, my sister, didn't have a jacket like mine. I ran outside, ready to cry, and climbed the tree by the alley to think bad thoughts and watch my breath puff white and disappear.

But whole pieces still casually flew off my jacket when I played hard, read quietly, or took vicious spelling tests at school. When it became so spotted that my brother began to call me "camouflage," I flung it over the fence into the alley. Later, however, I swiped the jacket off the ground and went inside to drape it across my lap and mope.

I was called to dinner: steam silvered my mother's glasses as she said grace; my brother and sister with their heads bowed made ugly faces at their glasses of powdered milk. I gagged too, but eagerly ate big rips of buttered tortilla that held scooped-up beans. Finished, I went outside with my jacket across my arm. It was a cold sky. The faces of clouds were piled up, hurting. I climbed the fence, jumping down with a grunt. I started up the alley and soon slipped into my jacket, that green ugly brother who breathed over my shoulder that day and ever since.

Key Terms

profile
hurled
swooping
braille
fleshy
palsied
camouflage

Questions on Meaning

1. According to Soto, what impact will the new jacket have on his life? Why is the size of the jacket so important to him?
2. How does Soto describe the reaction of others (boys, girls, teachers) to the jacket? Do you think that his description is accurate, or might it reflect his own feelings about the jacket? Explain your response.
3. Why does Soto blame all of the bad times of adolescence on his jacket? How common is such an explanation among young teenagers?

Questions on Rhetorical Strategy and Style

1. Soto uses the technique of comparison and contrast in describing the jacket he wanted with the one he received. How do the two jackets compare? What does each say about Soto's self-image?
2. Soto attributes many effects to the jacket; or, to put it another way, he sees the jacket as the cause of many bad things in his young life. Explain why you feel that he did or did not actually believe in a cause-and-effect relationship between the jacket and his misfortunes.
3. What is the effect of calling the jacket an "ugly brother"? How does this example of personification, or attributing human qualities to a non-human thing, help readers understand Soto's feelings about the jacket?

Writing Assignments

1. Write a brief essay describing an article of clothing that you disliked but were forced to wear. Using Soto as a model, focus on your initial reaction to the clothing, its impact on your life, and your feelings when you were finally rid of it.
2. Write a brief essay on the importance of clothes to adolescents. Consider such issues as the importance of brand names, the significance of looking different or similar to one's peers, the confidence (or lack of confidence) one feels with certain clothes, the relationship of clothes to sex appeal and/or to fitting in.

Black Men and Public Space

Brent Staples

Brent Staples (1951–) was born in Chester, Pennsylvania. He received his B. A. in behavioral sciences from Widener University in Chester and then his Ph.D. in psychology from the University of Chicago. He has worked as a writer for the Chicago Sun-Times, Chicago *magazine, and* Down Beat *magazine. He has written also for* New York Times Magazine, Ms., *and* Harper's. *Staples joined the editorial board of the* New York Times, *where he writes regularly on culture and politics. The following essay was first published in* Ms. *in 1986 and then in the revised version printed here in* Harper's *in 1987. In it Staples provides insight into a contemporary social phenomenon resulting from the racism and violence common in our world.*

1 My first victim was a woman—white, well dressed, probably 1
in her late twenties. I came upon her late one evening on a deserted street in Hyde Park, a relatively affluent neighborhood in an otherwise mean, impoverished section of Chicago. As I swung onto the avenue behind her, there seemed to be a discreet, uninflammatory distance between us. Not so. She cast back a worried glance. To her, the youngish black man—a broad six feet two inches with a beard and billowing hair, both hands shoved into the pockets of a bulky military jacket—seemed menacingly close. After a few more quick glimpses, she picked up her pace and was soon running in earnest. Within seconds she disappeared into a cross street.

That was more than a decade ago. I was twenty-two years old, a graduate student newly arrived at the University of Chicago. It was in the echo of that terrified woman's footfalls that I first began to know the unwieldy inheritance I'd come into—the ability to alter public space in ugly ways. It was clear that she thought herself the quarry of a mugger, a rapist, or worse. Suffering a bout of insomnia, however, I was stalking sleep, not defenseless wayfarers. As a softy who is scarcely able to take a knife to a raw chicken—let alone hold one to a person's throat—I was surprised, embarrassed, and dismayed all at once. Her flight made me feel like an accomplice in tyranny. It also made it clear that I was indistinguishable from the muggers who occasionally seeped into the area from the surrounding ghetto. That first encounter, and those that followed, signified that a vast, unnerving gulf lay between nighttime pedestrians—particularly women—and me. And I soon gathered that being perceived as dangerous is a hazard in itself. I only needed to turn a corner into a dicey situation, or crowd some frightened, armed person in a foyer somewhere, or make an errant move after being pulled over by a policeman. Where fear and weapons meet—and they often do in urban America—there is always the possibility of death.

In that first year, my first away from my hometown, I was to become thoroughly familiar with the language of fear. At dark, shadowy intersections, I could cross in front of a car stopped at a traffic light and elicit the *thunk, thunk, thunk, thunk* of the driver—black, white, male, or female—hammering down the door locks. On less traveled streets after dark, I grew accustomed to but never comfortable with people crossing to the other side of the street rather than pass me. Then there were the standard unpleasantries with policemen, doormen, bouncers, cabdrivers, and others whose business it is to screen out troublesome individuals *before* there is any nastiness.

I moved to New York nearly two years ago and I have remained an avid night walker. In central Manhattan, the near constant crowd cover minimizes tense one-on-one street encounters. Elsewhere—in SoHo, for example, where sidewalks are narrow and tightly spaced buildings shut out the sky—things can get very taut indeed.

5 After dark, on the warrenlike streets of Brooklyn where I live, I 5
often see women who fear the worst from me. They seem to have set their faces on neutral, and with their purse straps strung across their chests bandolier-style, they forge ahead as though bracing themselves

against being tackled. I understand, of course, that the danger they perceive is not a hallucination. Women are particularly vulnerable to street violence, and young black males are drastically overrepresented among the perpetrators of that violence. Yet these truths are no solace against the kind of alienation that comes of being ever the suspect, a fearsome entity with whom pedestrians avoid making eye contact.

It is not altogether clear to me how I reached the ripe old age of twenty-two without being conscious of the lethality nighttime pedestrians attributed to me. Perhaps it was because in Chester, Pennsylvania, the small, angry industrial town where I came of age in the 1960s, I was scarcely noticeable against a backdrop of gang warfare, street knifings, and murders. I grew up one of the good boys, had perhaps a half-dozen fistfights. In retrospect, my shyness of combat has clear sources.

As a boy, I saw countless tough guys locked away; I have since buried several, too. They were babies, really—a teenage cousin, a brother of twenty-two, a childhood friend in his mid-twenties—all gone down in episodes of bravado played out in the streets. I came to doubt the virtues of intimidation early on. I chose, perhaps unconsciously, to remain a shadow—timid, but a survivor.

The fearsomeness mistakenly attributed to me in public places often has a perilous flavor. The most frightening of these confusions occurred in the late 1970s and early 1980s, when I worked as a journalist in Chicago. One day, rushing into the office of a magazine I was writing for with a deadline story in hand, I was mistaken for a burglar. The office manager called security and, with an ad hoc posse, pursued me through the labyrinthine halls, nearly to my editor's door. I had no way of proving who I was. I could only move briskly toward the company of someone who knew me.

Another time I was on assignment for a local paper and killing time before an interview. I entered a jewelry store on the city's affluent Near North Side. The proprietor excused herself and returned with an enormous red Doberman pinscher straining at the end of a leash. She stood, the dog extended toward me, silent to my questions, her eyes bulging nearly out of her head. I took a cursory look around, nodded, and bade her good night.

10 Relatively speaking, however, I never fared as badly as another 10
black male journalist. He went to nearby Waukegan, Illinois, a couple of summers ago to work on a story about a murderer who was born

there. Mistaking the reporter for the killer, police officers hauled him from his car at gunpoint and but for his press credentials would probably have tried to book him. Such episodes are not uncommon. Black men trade tales like this all the time.

Over the years, I learned to smother the rage I felt at so often being taken for a criminal. Not to do so would surely have led to madness. I now take precautions to make myself less threatening. I move about with care, particularly late in the evening. I give a wide berth to nervous people on subway platforms during the wee hours, particularly when I have exchanged business clothes for jeans. If I happen to be entering a building behind some people who appear skittish, I may walk by, letting them clear the lobby before I return, so as not to seem to be following them. I have been calm and extremely congenial on those rare occasions when I've been pulled over by the police.

And on late-evening constitutionals I employ what has proved to be an excellent tension-reducing measure: I whistle melodies from Beethoven and Vivaldi and the more popular classical composers. Even steely New Yorkers hunching toward nighttime destinations seem to relax, and occasionally they even join in the tune. Virtually everybody seems to sense that a mugger wouldn't be warbling bright, sunny selections from Vivaldi's *Four Seasons.* It is my equivalent of the cowbell that hikers wear when they know they are in bear country.

Questions on Meaning

1. Does Staples blame the people who fear him on the street at night? Does he explain the source of the societal problem he describes?
2. Staples says he has "learned to smother the rage I felt at so often being taken for a criminal"—but clearly he has not forgotten his pain and anger. How would you describe his attitude now toward this reality in our society?
3. In addition to being black and male, what about Staples might lead to some people feeling afraid to have him walking behind them on a quiet street at night? To what extent does Staples discuss these other factors? To what extent do you feel some women might react similarly to a large white man dressed in a military jacket walking behind them on a quiet street at night? Comment on what is different, however, about being black in this circumstance.

Questions on Rhetorical Strategy and Style

1. Much of the power of this essay comes from the many examples Staples gives of the phenomenon he is writing about. Choose two examples of how his presence affected others in public space and analyze them phrase by phrase, image by image, to see how his writing has this impact.
2. Analyze Staples' style. Pay attention to both the colloquial, conversational language of phrases such as "a dicey situation" and the more formal language of his sociological observations. Make a list of words that describe his style.

Writing Assignments

1. Most of us, male or female, black or white, have been in situations in which we felt like Staples' "victim"—in the presence of someone we interpreted as a threat to our well-being. Looking back at such situations and fears, after having read this essay, do you now think you were justified in your fear? Would you now wonder, in the same circumstances, whether you might be offending the person by reacting with fear? Or, not knowing anything more about the person, are you still in a better position reacting as if the person *is* a threat? What do you think Staples would advise you to do in such a situation?

2. It has been said that it is natural to fear the unknown. Do you see this as a clear cause-effect relationship? Think of circumstances in which you would fear something or someone unknown. Try to define the characteristics that would lead to fear. Then write an essay in which you explain your thoughts on the relationship between the unknown and fear.

Miss U.S.A.

Studs Terkel

Studs Terkel (1912–2008) was a writer whose style resembles that of another roughhewn Chicago journalist, the late Mike Royko. Terkel acted on stage and television, hosted a radio program, and compiled books of his interviews. Among his books are Division Street America *(1967),* Hard Times *(1970),* Working *(1974),* American Dreams: Lost and Found *(1980) the Pulitzer prize-winning* The Good War: An Oral History of World War Two *(1984),* Chicago *(1986), and* The Great Divide *(1988). Terkel represented class conflict in a deceptively simple journalistic style, allowing the facts and the people he interviewed to speak for themselves, as in this selection taken from* American Dreams.

Emma Knight, Miss U.S.A., 1973. She is twenty-nine.

1 I wince when I'm called a former beauty queen or Miss U.S.A. I keep thinking they're talking about someone else. There are certain images that come to mind when people talk about beauty queens. It's mostly what's known as t and a, tits and ass. No talent. For many girls who enter the contest, it's part of the American Dream. It was never mine. 1

You used to sit around the TV and watch Miss America and it was exciting, we thought, glamorous. Fun, we thought. But by the time I was eight or nine, I didn't feel comfortable. Soon I'm hitting my adolescence, like fourteen, but I'm not doing any dating and I'm feeling awkward and ugly. I'm much taller than most of the people in my class. I don't feel I can compete the way I see girls competing for guys. I was very much of a loner. I felt intimidated by the amount of competition

---

From *American Dreams: Lost and Found* (New York: Pantheon Books, 1980). Copyright © 1980 by Studs Terkel.

females were supposed to go through with each other. I didn't like being told by *Seventeen* magazine: Subvert your interests if you have a crush on a guy, get interested in what he's interested in. If you play cards, be sure not to beat him. I was very bad at these social games.

After I went to the University of Colorado for three and a half years, I had it. This was 1968 through '71. I came home for the summer. An agent met me and wanted me to audition for commercials, modeling, acting jobs. Okay. I started auditioning and winning some.

I did things actors do when they're starting out. You pass out literature at conventions, you do print ads, you pound the pavements, you send out your resumés. I had come to a model agency one cold day, and an agent came out and said: "I want you to enter a beauty contest." I said: "No, uh-uh, never, never, never. I'll lose, how humiliating." She said: "I want some girls to represent the agency, might do you good." So I filled out the application blank: hobbies, measurements, blah, blah, blah. I got a letter: "Congratulations. You have been accepted as an entrant into the Miss Illinois-Universe contest." Now what do I do? I'm stuck.

You have to have a sponsor. Or you're gonna have to pay several hundred dollars. So I called up the lady who was running it. Terribly sorry, I can't do this. I don't have the money. She calls back a couple of days later: "We found you a sponsor, it's a lumber company."

It was in Decatur. There were sixty-some contestants from all over the place. I went as a lumberjack: blue jeans, hiking boots, a flannel shirt, a pair of suspenders, and carrying an axe. You come out first in your costume and you introduce yourself and say your astrological sign or whatever it is they want you to say. You're wearing a banner that has the sponsor's name on it. Then you come out and do your pirouettes in your one-piece bathing suit, and the judges look at you a lot. Then you come out in your evening gown and pirouette around for a while. That's the first night.

The second night, they're gonna pick fifteen people. In between, you had judges' interviews. For three minutes, they ask you anything they want. Can you answer questions? How do you handle yourself? Your poise, personality, blah, blah, blah. They're called personality judges.

I thought: This will soon be over, get on a plane tomorrow, and no one will be the wiser. Except that my name got called as one of the fifteen. You have to go through the whole thing all over again.

I'm thinking: I don't have a prayer. I'd come to feel a certain kind of distance, except that they called my name. I was the winner, Miss Illinois. All I could do was laugh. I'm twenty-two, standing up there in a borrowed evening gown, thinking: What am I doing here: This is like Tom Sawyer becomes an altar boy.

10 I was considered old for a beauty queen, which is a little horrify- 10
ing when you're twenty-two. That's very much part of the beauty queen syndrome: the young, untouched, unthinking human being.

I had to go to this room and sign the Miss Illinois-Universe contract right away. Miss Universe, Incorporated, is the full name of the company. It's owned by Kayser-Roth, Incorporated, which was bought out by Gulf & Western. Big business.

I'm sitting there with my glass of champagne and I'm reading over this contract. They said: "Oh, you don't have to read it." And I said: "I never sign anything that I don't read." They're all waiting to take pictures, and I'm sitting there reading this long document. So I signed it and the phone rang and the guy was from a Chicago paper and said: "Tell me, is it Miss or Ms.?" I said: "It's Ms." He said: "You're kidding." I said: "No, I'm not." He wrote an article the next day saying something like it finally happened: a beauty queen, a feminist. I thought I was a feminist before I was a beauty queen, why should I stop now?

Then I got into the publicity and training and interviews. It was a throwback to another time where crossed ankles and white gloves and teacups were present. I was taught how to walk around with a book on my head, how to sit daintily, how to pose in a bathing suit, and how to frizz my hair. They wanted curly hair, which I hate.

One day the trainer asked me to shake hands. I shook hands. She said: "That's wrong. When you shake hands with a man, you always shake hands ring up." I said: "Like the pope? Where my hand is up, like he's gonna kiss it?" Right. I thought: Holy mackerel! It was a very long February and March and April and May.

15 I won the Miss U.S.A. pageant. I started to laugh. They tell me 15
I'm the only beauty queen in history that didn't cry when she won. It was on network television. I said to myself: "You're kidding." Bob Barker, the host, said: "No, I'm not kidding." I didn't know what else to say at that moment. In the press releases, they call it the great American Dream. There she is, Miss America, your ideal. Well, not my ideal, kid.

The minute you're crowned, you become their property and subject to whatever they tell you. They wake you up at seven o'clock next morning and make you put on a negligee and serve you breakfast in bed, so that all the New York papers can come in and take your picture sitting in bed, while you're absolutely bleary-eyed from the night before. They put on the Kayser-Roth negligee, hand you the tray, you take three bites. The photographers leave, you whip off the negligee, they take the breakfast away, and that's it. I never did get any breakfast that day. (Laughs).

You immediately start making personal appearances. The Jaycees or the chamber of commerce says: "I want to book Miss U.S.A. for our Christmas Day parade." They pay, whatever it is, seven hundred fifty dollars a day, first-class air fare, round trip, expenses, so forth. If the United Fund calls and wants me to give a five-minute pitch on queens at a luncheon, they still have to pay a fee. Doesn't matter that it's a charity. It's one hundred percent to Miss Universe, Incorporated. You get your salary. That's your prize money for the year. I got fifteen thousand dollars, which is all taxed in New York. Maybe out of a check of three thousand dollars, I'd get fifteen hundred dollars.

From the day I won Miss U.S.A. to the day I left for Universe, almost two months, I got a day and a half off. I made about two hundred fifty appearances that year. Maybe three hundred. Parades, shopping centers, and things. Snip ribbons. What else do you do at a shopping center? Model clothes. The nice thing I got to do was public speaking. They said: "You want a ghost writer?" I said: "Hell, no, I know how to talk." I wrote my own speeches. They don't trust girls to go out and talk because most of them can't.

One of the big execs from General Motors asked me to do a speech in Washington, D.C., on the consumer and the energy crisis. It was the fiftieth anniversary of the National Management Association. The White House, for some reason, sent me some stuff on it. I read it over, it was nonsense. So I stood up and said: "The reason we have an energy crisis is because we are, industrially and personally, pigs. We have a short-term view of the resources available to us; and unless we wake up to what we're doing to our air and our water, we'll have a dearth, not just a crisis." Oh, they weren't real pleased. (Laughs.)

What I resent most is that a lot of people didn't expect me to live this version of the American Dream for myself. I was supposed to live it their way.

When it came out in a newspaper interview that I said Nixon should resign, that he was a crook, oh dear, the fur flew. They got very upset until I got an invitation to the White House. They wanted to shut me up. The Miss Universe corporation had been trying to establish some sort of liaison with the White House for several years. I make anti-Nixon speeches and get this invitation.

I figured they're either gonna take me down to the basement and beat me up with a rubber hose or they're gonna offer me a cabinet post. They had a list of fifteen or so people I was supposed to meet. I've never seen such a bunch of people with raw nerve endings. I was dying to bring a tape recorder but thought if you mention the word "Sony" in the Nixon White House, you're in trouble. They'd have cardiac arrest. But I'm gonna bring along a pad and paper. They were patronizing. And when one of 'em got me in his office and talked about all the journalists and television people being liberals, I brought up blacklisting, *Red Channels,* and the TV industry. He changed the subject.

Miss Universe took place in Athens, Greece. The junta was still in power. I saw a heck of a lot of jeeps and troops and machine guns. The Americans were supposed to keep a low profile. I had never been a great fan of the Greek junta, but I knew darn well I was gonna have to keep my mouth shut. I was still representing the United States, for better or for worse. Miss Philippines won. I ran second.

At the end of the year, you're run absolutely ragged. That final evening, they usually have several queens from past years come back. Before they crown the new Miss U.S.A., the current one is supposed to take what they call the farewell walk. They call over the PA: Time for the old queen's walk. I'm now twenty-three and I'm an old queen. And they have this idiot farewell speech playing over the airwaves as the old queen takes the walk. And you're sitting on the throne for about thirty seconds, then you come down and they announce the name of the new one and you put the crown on her head. And then you're old.

As the new one is crowned, the reporters and photographers rush on the stage. I've seen photographers shove the girl who has just given her reign up thirty seconds before, shove her physically. I was gone by that time. I had jumped off the stage in my evening gown. It is very difficult for girls who are terrified of this ending. All of a sudden (snaps fingers), you're out. Nobody gives a damn about the old one.

Miss U.S.A. and remnants thereof is the crown stored in the attic in my parents' home. I don't even know where the banners are. It wasn't me the fans of Miss U.S.A. thought was pretty. What they think is pretty is the banner and crown. If I could put the banner and crown on that lamp, I swear to God ten men would come in and ask it for a date. I'll think about committing an axe murder if I'm not called anything but a former beauty queen. I can't stand it any more.

Several times during my year as what's-her-face I had seen the movie *The Sting.* There's a gesture the characters use which means the con is on: they rub their nose. In my last fleeting moments as Miss U.S.A., as they were playing that silly farewell speech and I walked down the aisle and stood by the throne, I looked right into the camera and rubbed my finger across my nose. The next day, the pageant people spent all their time telling people that I hadn't done it. I spent the time telling them that, of course, I had. I simply meant: the con is on. (Laughs.)

Miss U.S.A. is in the same graveyard that Emma Knight the twelve-year-old is. Where the sixteen-year-old is. All the past selves. There comes a time when you have to bury those selves because you've grown into another one. You don't keep exhuming the corpses.

If I could sit down with every young girl in America for the next fifty years, I could tell them what I liked about the pageant. I could tell them what I hated. It wouldn't make any difference. There're always gonna be girls who want to enter the beauty pageant. That's the fantasy: the American Dream.

Key Terms

wince
subvert
pirouette
feminist
negligee
dearth
patronizing
blacklisting

Questions on Meaning

1. Were you surprised by some of what Emma Knight had to say? What were your prior assumptions about beauty queens and how did Knight's attitudes change them?
2. Knight clearly feels that she was exploited as a beauty queen. Do you agree that women can be exploited in this way? Explain your response.
3. Knight was a Miss U.S.A. contestant in 1973. Do you feel that beauty contests have changed since then? Check your impression with someone who remembers these contests from decades ago.

Questions on Rhetorical Strategy and Style

1. This selection is an example of a profile. Terkel is famous for his profiles. The speaker in the narrative, however, is Knight. What is Terkel's role in shaping this profile and its point of view?
2. Why does the selection open with "I wince when I'm called a former beauty queen or Miss U.S.A."? What tone does this statement establish with the reader?
3. The purpose of a profile is to leave the reader with a dominant impression of its subject, in this case Knight. What impression do you have of her? Which details most convey that impression?

Writing Assignments

1. Profiles are a common form of writing. Most often magazines publish profiles of celebrities. However, they are also written about more everyday people. Sometimes they are called human interest stories. Write a profile of a person who is interesting to you. You can gather material about your subject by observing him or her doing something meaningful and through interviews.
2. Recently there have been some criticisms of beauty contests, especially since they have become popular as contest for little girls. With so much media display of women in our society today, why have beauty contests come under attack? Write a brief opinion piece on this issue.

The Ethic of Compassion

The Dalai Lama

His Holiness the Dalai Lama (1935–) was born a peasant in Taktser, Tibet under the birth name of Lhamo Dhondrub. He is the fourteenth Dalai Lama (spiritual leader of Tibet, reincarnation of the thirteenth Dalai Lama, and an incarnation of the Buddha of Compassion). He lives in Dharamsala, India. He was recognized at age two as the Dalai Lama and was enthroned on February 22, 1940. He completed the Geshe Lharampa Degree (equivalent to a Doctorate of Buddhist Philosophy) in 1959 and became head of Tibet—but was driven out by a Chinese invasion. He has worked on behalf of Tibet from India, asking the United Nations for help and working to bring Buddhist beliefs back to the country. He received the Albert Schweitzer Humanitarian Award (1987); Raoul Wallenberg Congressional Human Rights Award (1989); the Nobel Peace Prize (1989); Franklin D. Roosevelt Freedom Medal (1994); and the Hessian Peace Prize (2005). His books include Kindness, Clarity and Insight *(Snow Lion, 1984);* Compassion and the Individual *(Wisdom Publications, 1991); and* The Power of Compassion *(Harper Collins, 1995).*

Compassion is good when first considered, for it is easy to feel compassion for one who suffers. Compassion is harder to muster for wealthy and powerful people and even harder to feel when true compassion leads to a career change or an even greater life upheaval.

1 We noted earlier that all the world's major religions stress the 1
importance of cultivating love and compassion. In the Buddhist philosophical tradition, different levels of attainment

are described. At a basic level, compassion (*nying je*) is understood mainly in terms of empathy—our ability to enter into and, to some extent, share others' suffering. But Buddhist—and perhaps others—believe that this can be developed to such a degree that not only does our compassion arise without any effort, but it is unconditional, undifferentiated, and universal in scope. A feeling of intimacy toward all other sentient beings, including of course those who would harm us, is generated, which is likened in the literature to the love a mother has for her only child.

But this sense of equanimity toward all others is not seen as an end in itself. Rather, it is seen as the springboard to a love still greater. Because our capacity for empathy is innate, and because the ability to reason is also an innate faculty, compassion shares the characteristics of consciousness itself. The potential we have to develop it is therefore stable and continuous. It is not a resource which can be used up—as water is used up when we boil it. And though it can be described in terms of activity, it is not like a physical activity which we train for, like jumping, where once we reach a certain height we can go no further. On the contrary, when we enhance our sensitivity toward others' suffering through deliberately opening ourselves up to it, it is believed that we can gradually extend out compassion to the point where the individual feels so moved by even the subtlest suffering of others that they come to have an over-whelming sense of responsibility toward those others. This causes the one who is compassionate to dedicate themselves entirely to helping others overcome both their suffering and the causes of their suffering. In Tibetan, this ultimate level of attainment is called *nying je chenmo,* literally "great compassion."

Now I am not suggesting that each individual must attain these advanced states of spiritual development in order to lead an ethically wholesome life. I have described *nying je chenmo* not because it is a precondition of ethical conduct but rather because I believe that pushing the logic of compassion to the highest level can act as a powerful inspiration. If we can just keep the aspiration to develop *nying je chenmo,* or great compassion, as an ideal, it will naturally have a significant impact on our outlook. Based on the simple recognition that, just as I do, so do all others desire to be happy and not to suffer, it will serve as a constant reminder against selfishness and partiality. It will remind us that there is little to be gained from being kind and generous because we hope to win something in return. It will remind us that actions motivated by the desire to create a good name for ourselves are still selfish, however much they may appear to be acts of kindness. It will also remind us that there is nothing exceptional about acts of charity toward those we already feel close to. And it will help us to recognize that the bias we naturally feel toward our families and friends is actually a highly unreliable thing on which to base ethical conduct. If we reserve ethical conduct for those whom we feel close to, the danger is that we will neglect our responsibilities toward those outside this circle.

Why is this? So long as the individuals in question continue to meet our expectations, all is well. But should they fail to do so, someone we consider a dear friend one day can become our sworn enemy the next. As we saw earlier, we have a tendency to react badly to all who threaten fulfillment of our cherished desires, though they may be our closest relations. For this reason, compassion and mutual respect offer a much more solid basis for our relations with others. This is also true of partnerships. If our love for someone is based largely on attraction, whether it be their looks or some other superficial characteristic, our feelings for that person are liable, over time, to evaporate. When they lose the quality we found alluring, or when we find ourselves no longer satisfied by it, the situation can change completely, this despite their being the same person. This is why relationships based purely on attraction are almost always unstable. On the other hand, when we begin to perfect our compassion, neither the other's appearance nor their behavior affects our underlying attitude.

Consider, too, that habitually our feelings toward others depend very much on their circumstances. Most people, when they see someone who is handicapped, feel sympathetic toward that person. But then when they see others who are wealthier, or better educated, or better placed socially, they immediately feel envious and competitive toward them. Our negative feelings prevent us from seeing the sameness of ourselves and all others. We forget that just like us, whether fortunate or unfortunate, distant or near, they desire to be happy and not to suffer.

The struggle is thus to overcome these feelings of partiality. Certainly, developing genuine compassion for our loved ones is the obvious and appropriate place to start. The impact our actions have on our close ones will generally be much greater than on others, and therefore our responsibilities toward them are greater. Yet we need to recognize that, ultimately, there are no grounds for discriminating in their favor. In this sense, we are all in the same position as a doctor confronted by ten patients suffering the same serious illness. They are each equally deserving of treatment. The reader should not suppose that what is being advocated here is a state of detached indifference, however. The further essential challenge, as we begin to extend our compassion toward all others, is to maintain the same level of intimacy as we feel toward those closest to us. In other words, what is being suggested is that we need to strive for even-handedness in our approach toward all others, a level ground into which we can plant the seed of *nying je chenmo,* of great love and compassion.

If we can begin to relate to others on the basis of such equanimity, our compassion will not depend on the fact that so and so is my husband, my wife, my relative, my friend. Rather, a feeling of closeness toward all others can be developed based on the simple recognition that, just like myself, all wish to be happy and to avoid suffering. In other words, we will start to relate to others on the basis of their sentient nature. Again, we can think of this in terms of an ideal, one which it is immensely difficult to attain. But, for myself, I find it one which is profoundly inspiring and helpful.

Let us now consider the role of compassionate love and kindheartedness in our daily lives. Does the ideal of developing it to the point where it is unconditional mean that we must abandon our own interests entirely? Not at all. In fact, it is the best way of serving them—indeed, it could even be said to constitute the wisest course for fulfilling self-interest. For if it is correct that those qualities such as love, patience, tolerance, and forgiveness are what happiness consists in, and if it is also correct that *nying je,* or compassion, as I have defined it, is both the source and the fruit of these qualities, then the more we are compassionate, the more we provide for our own happiness. Thus, any idea that concern for others, though a noble quality, is a matter for our private lives only, is simply short-sighted. Compassion belongs to every sphere of activity, including, of course, the workplace.

Here, though, I must acknowledge the existence of a perception—shared by many, it seems—that compassion is, if not actually an impediment, at least irrelevant to professional life. Personally, I would argue that not only is it relevant, but that when compassion is lacking, our activities are in danger of becoming destructive. This is because when we ignore the question of the impact our actions have on others' well-being, inevitably we end up hurting them. The ethic of compassion helps provide the necessary foundation and motivation for both restraint and the cultivation of virtue. When we begin to develop a genuine appreciation of the value of compassion, our outlook on others begins automatically to change. This alone can serve as a powerful influence on the conduct of our lives. When, for example, the temptation to deceive others arises, our compassion for them will prevent us from entertaining the idea. And when we realize that our work itself is in danger of being exploited to the detriment of others, compassion will cause us to disengage from it. So to take an imaginary case of a scientist whose research seems likely to be a source of suffering, they will recognize this and act accordingly, even if this means abandoning the project.

I do not deny that genuine problems can arise when we dedicate ourselves to the ideal of compassion. In the case of a scientist who felt unable to continue in the direction their work was taking them, this could have profound consequences both for themselves and for their families. Likewise, those engaged in the caring professions—in medicine, counseling, social work, and so on—or even those looking after someone at home may sometimes become so exhausted by their duties that they feel overwhelmed. Constant exposure to suffering, coupled occasionally with a feeling of being taken for granted, can induce feelings of helplessness and even despair. Or it can happen that individuals may find themselves performing outwardly generous actions merely for the sake of it—simply going through the motions, as it were. Of course this is better than nothing. But when left unchecked, this can lead to insensitivity toward others' suffering. If this starts to happen, it is best to disengage for a short while and make a deliberate effort to reawaken that sensitivity. In this it can be helpful to remember that despair is never a solution. It is, rather, the ultimate failure. Therefore, as the Tibetan expression has it, even if the rope breaks nine times, we must splice it back together a tenth time. In this way, even if ultimately we do fail, at least there will be no feelings of regret. And when we combine this insight with a clear appreciation of our potential to benefit others, we find that we can begin to restore our hope and confidence.

Some people may object to this ideal on the grounds that by entering into others' suffering, we bring suffering on ourselves. To an extent, this is true. But I suggest that there is an important qualitative distinction to be made between experiencing one's own suffering and experiencing suffering in the course of sharing in others'. In the case of one's own suffering, given that it is involuntary, there is a sense of oppression: it seems to come from outside us. By contrast, sharing in someone else's suffering must at some level involve a degree of voluntariness, which itself is indicative of a certain inner strength. For this reason, the disturbance it may cause is considerably less likely to paralyze us than our own suffering.

Of course, even as an ideal, the notion of developing unconditional compassion is daunting. Most people, including myself, must struggle even to reach the point where putting others' interests on a par with our own becomes easy. We should not allow this to put us off, however. And while undoubtedly there will be obstacles on the way to developing a genuinely warm heart, there is the deep consolation of knowing that in doing so we are creating the conditions for our own happiness. As I mentioned earlier, the more we truly desire to benefit others, the greater the strength and confidence we develop and the greater the peace and happiness we experience. If this still seems unlikely, it is worth asking ourselves how else we are to do so. With violence and aggression? Of course not. With money? Perhaps up to a point, but no further. But with love, by sharing in others' suffering, by recognizing ourselves clearly in all others—especially those who are disadvantaged and those whose rights are not respected—by helping them to, be happy: yes. Through love, through kindness, through compassion we establish understanding between ourselves and others. This is how we forge unity and harmony.

Compassion and love are not mere luxuries. As the source both of inner and external peace, they are fundamental to the continued survival of our species. On the one hand, they constitute non-violence in action. On the other, they are the source of all spiritual qualities: of forgiveness, tolerance, and all the virtues. Moreover, they are the very thing that gives meaning to our activities and makes them constructive. There is nothing amazing about being highly educated; there is nothing amazing about being rich. Only when the individual has a warm heart do these attributes become worthwhile.

So to those who say that the Dalai Lama is being unrealistic in advocating this ideal of unconditional love, I urge them to experiment with it nonetheless. They will discover that when we reach beyond the confines of narrow self-interest, our hearts become filled with strength. Peace and joy become our constant companion. It breaks down barriers of every kind and in the end destroys the notion of my interest as independent from others' interest. But most important, so far as ethics is concerned, where love of one's neighbor, affection, kindness, and compassion live, we find that ethical conduct is automatic. Ethically wholesome actions arise naturally in the context of compassion.

Questions on Meaning

1. Compassion means to empathize with another, to feel that person's joy, pain, and hope. Why does the author say that feeling compassion for the disabled or the poor is easy? Why is it hard to feel sympathy for those we envy?
2. What would happen to our ordinary, selfish lives if we were to start feeling real compassion? Would we be able to use the environment and the rest of the world as we do now? What would we have to change?
3. What does the individual gain by feeling compassion? Is the kind of peace and love that are described in this essay really what people want? Why do most of us live lives that are aimed at making money and winning, rather than loving?

Questions on Rhetorical Strategy and Style

1. The tone of this essay is very gentle and kind, but the message is quite tough. How does the author warn the reader in the introduction that the essay is going to be demanding and maybe a bit disturbing?
2. The essay moves to a cause and effect structure: If one feels true compassion, the feeling may cause one to have to change one's life. The feeling, though a good one, may lead to uncomfortable results. How does this causality affect the reader of the essay? Is a reader likely to change behavior in light of this cause and effect explanation?
3. The end of the essay promises that great good can come from feeling compassion. How does the writer hope to persuade the reader that these benefits are worthwhile? Does this ending promise better things for the world if many readers are persuaded? Is it even possible?

Writing Assignments

1. A wise person once said that we should feel compassion rather than guilt, for we will act from compassion, but we will merely suffer from guilt. Think of someone you know whom you consider compassionate. Write about what that person does with life. What kind of work does the person do? What kind of entertainment and leisure activities does that person pursue?

2. Write about a world leader whom you consider compassionate. Show how this feeling is displayed in the person's actions. What would happen to world politics if everyone acted with compassion?
3. Consider a world conflict, either one occurring now or one in history. Write about how the events could be or would have been different had the parties shown more compassion and less aggression.

The Baffling Question

Bill Cosby

Bill Cosby (1937–) dropped out of high school and entered the Navy, but eventually attended Temple University on a football scholarship and, upon graduation, began doing standup comedy. A series of Grammy-winning comedy records and hit movies and television shows followed, much of the comedy based on the commonplaces of family life. His fame as a symbol of American family life reached its peak in the 1980s when his weekly situation comedy, The Cosby Show (1984–1992), had an audience of sixty million viewers. In the essay printed below, an excerpt from his book Fatherhood *(1986), you can detect the influence of the patterns of spoken English in the pacing and development of ideas that were incorporated in comedy routines.*

1 So you've decided to have a child. You've decided to give up quiet 1
evenings with good books and lazy weekends with good music, intimate meals during which you finish whole sentences, sweet private times when you've savored the thought that just the two of you and your love are all you will ever need. You've decided to turn your sofas into trampolines and to abandon the joys of leisurely contemplating reproductions of great art for the joys of frantically coping with reproductions of yourselves.

Why?

Poets have said the reason to have children is to give yourself immortality; and I must admit I did ask God to give me a son because I wanted someone to carry on the family name. Well, God did just that and I now confess that there have been times when I've told my son not to reveal who he is.

"You make up a name," I've said. "Just don't tell anybody who you are.

Immortality? Now that I have had five children, my only hope is that they all are out of the house before I die.

No, immortality was not the reason why my wife and I produced these beloved sources of dirty laundry and ceaseless noise. And we also did not have them because we thought it would be fun to see one of them sit in a chair and stick out his leg so that another one of them running by was launched like Explorer I. After which I said to the child who was the launching pad, "Why did you do that?"

"Do what?" he replied.

"Stick out your leg."

"Dad, I didn't know my leg was going out. My leg, it does that a lot."

If you cannot function in a world where things like this are said, then you better forget about raising children and go for daffodils. My wife and I also did not have children so they could yell at each other all over the house, moving me to say, "What's the problem?"

"She's waving her foot in my room," my daughter replied.

"And something like that *bothers* you?"

"Yes, I don't *want* her foot in my room."

"Well," I said, dipping into my storehouse of paternal wisdom, why don't you just close the door?"

"Then I can't see what she's doing!"

Furthermore, we did not have the children because we thought it would be rewarding to watch them do things that should be studied by the Menninger Clinic.

"Okay," I said to all five one day, "go get into the car."

All five then ran to the same car door, grabbed the same handle, and spent the next few minutes beating each other up. Not one of them had the intelligence to say, "Hey, *look.* There are three more doors." The dog, however, was already inside.

And we did not have the children to help my wife develop new lines for her face or because she had always had a desire to talk out loud to herself. "Don't tell *me* you're *not* going to do something when I tell you to move!" And we didn't have children so I could always be saying to someone, "Where's my change?"

Like so many young couples, my wife and I simply were unable to project. In restaurants we did not see the small children who were casting their bread on the water in the glasses the waiter had brought; and we did not see the mother who was fasting because she was both cutting the food for one child while pulling another from the floor to a chair that he would use for slipping to the floor again. And we did not project beyond those lovely Saturdays of buying precious little things after leisurely brunches together. We did not see that *other* precious little things would be coming along to destroy the first batch.

Key Terms

intimate
savored
contemplating
immortality
storehouse
paternal
project (verb)

Questions on Meaning

1. What reasons does Cosby offer for having children? What reasons does he offer for *not* having children?
2. Based on Cosby's perspective, how would you describe the typical child?

Questions on Rhetorical Strategy and Style

1. Cosby writes this essay using second person (you) and first person (I). Why do you suppose he chose this approach rather than using third person (he/she/they)? How does this choice affect his relationship to his readers?
2. In the middle of the essay, Cosby uses dialogue in explaining his children's behavior. How would the impact of these passages have been different had he simply described these incidents? Read the dialogue aloud. How does the dialogue contribute to the humor of the essay?

Writing Assignments

1. Using Cosby as a model, write a humorous essay about a choice you think people should not make (e.g., going to college, buying a used car, becoming engaged). Try to create scenes, as Cosby does, to emphasize your point.
2. Cosby describes children from the point of view of parents. Write an essay that describes parents from the point of view of children. Using Cosby's style as a model, recreate several incidents to illustrate your point.

Beauty: When the Other Dancer Is the Self

Alice Walker

Alice Walker (1944–) was born in Georgia to sharecropper parents. She attended Spelman College and Sarah Lawrence College and was active in the civil rights movement of the 1960s. Publishing her first novel, The Third Life of Grange Copeland, *at the age of 26, she has been a prolific writer since. In all, she has published five novels, two short story collections, two collections of essays, and several books of poems. Her novel* The Color Purple *(1982) is perhaps her best known, having won the American Book Award, the Pulitzer Prize, and the Candace Award of the National Coalition of 100 Black Women. The novel was also made into a prize-winning film by director Steven Spielberg. Walker's topics run the gamut of human experience and include some harsh realities such as incest and racial violence as well as relationships within families and society. In the following essay, published in* In Search of Our Mothers' Gardens: Womanist Prose *(1983), Walker examines an important aspect of her childhood that, while more personal than social, appears in an inevitable context of poorer blacks in the rural South.*

1 It is a bright summer day in 1947. My father, a fat, funny man with 1
beautiful eyes and a subversive wit, is trying to decide which of his eight children he will take with him to the county fair. My mother, of course, will not go. She is knocked out from getting most of us ready: I hold my neck stiff against the pressure of her knuckles as she hastily completes the braiding and then be-ribboning of my hair.

My father is the driver for the rich old white lady up the road. Her name is Miss Mey. She owns all the land for miles around, as well as the house in which we live. All I remember about her is that she once offered to pay my mother thirty-five cents for cleaning her house, raking up piles of her magnolia leaves, and washing her family's clothes, and that my mother—she of no money, eight children, and a chronic earache—refused it. But I do not think of this in 1947. I am two and a half years old. I want to go everywhere my daddy goes. I am excited at the prospect of riding in a car. Someone has told me fairs are fun. That there is room in the car for only three of us doesn't faze me at all. Whirling happily in my starchy frock, showing off my biscuit-polished patent-leather shoes and lavender socks, tossing my head in a way that makes my ribbons bounce, I stand, hands on hips, before my father. "Take me, Daddy," I say with assurance; "I'm the prettiest!"

Later, it does not surprise me to find myself in Miss Mey's shiny black car, sharing the back seat with the other lucky ones. Does not surprise me that I thoroughly enjoy the fair. At home that night I tell the unlucky ones all I can remember about the merry-go-round, the man who eats live chickens, and the teddy bears, until they say: that's enough, baby Alice. Shut up now, and go to sleep.

It is Easter Sunday, 1950. I am dressed in a green, flocked, scalloped-hem dress (handmade by my adoring sister, Ruth) that has its own smooth satin petticoat and tiny hot-pink roses tucked into each scallop. My shoes, new T-strap patent leather, again highly biscuit-polished. I am six years old and have learned one of the longest Easter speeches to be heard that day, totally unlike the speech I said when I was two: "Easter lilies / pure and white / blossom in / the morning light." When I rise to give my speech I do so on a great wave of love and pride and expectation. People in the church stop rustling their new crinolines. They seem to hold their breath. I can tell they admire my dress, but it is my spirit, bordering on sassiness (womanishness), they secretly applaud.

5 "That girl's a little *mess,*" they whisper to each other, pleased.

Naturally I say my speech without stammer or pause, unlike those who stutter, stammer, or, worst of all, forget. This is before the word "beautiful" exists in people's vocabulary, but "Oh, isn't she the *cutest* thing!" frequently floats my way. "And got so much sense!" they gratefully add . . . for which thoughtful addition I thank them to this day.

It was great fun being cute. But then, one day, it ended.

I am eight years old and a tomboy. I have a cowboy hat, cowboy boots, checkered shirt and pants, all red. My playmates are my brothers, two and four years older than I. Their colors are black and green, the only difference in the way we are dressed. On Saturday nights we all go to the picture show, even my mother; Westerns are her favorite kind of movie. Back home, "on the ranch," we pretend we are Tom Mix, Hopalong Cassidy, Lash LaRue (we've even named one of our dogs Lash LaRue); we chase each other for hours rustling cattle, being outlaws, delivering damsels from distress. Then my parents decide to buy my brothers guns. These are not "real" guns. They shoot "BBs," copper pellets my brothers say will kill birds. Because I am a girl, I do not get a gun. Instantly I am relegated to the position of Indian. Now there appears a great distance between us. They shoot and shoot at everything with their new guns. I try to keep up with my bow and arrows.

One day while I am standing on top of our makeshift "garage"—pieces of tin nailed across some poles—holding my bow and arrow and looking out toward the fields, I feel an incredible blow in my right eye. I look down just in time to see my brother lower his gun.

10 Both brothers rush to my side. My eye stings, and I cover it with my hand. "If you tell," they say, "we will get a whipping. You don't want that to happen, do you?" I do not. "Here is a piece of wire," says the older brother, picking it up from the roof; "say you stepped on one end of it and the other flew up and hit you." The pain is beginning to start. "Yes," I say. "Yes, I will say that is what happened." If I do not say this is what happened, I know my brothers will find ways to make me wish I had. But now I will say anything that gets me to my mother. 10

Confronted by our parents we stick to the lie agreed upon. They place me on a bench on the porch and I close my left eye while they examine the right. There is a tree growing from underneath the porch that climbs past the railing to the roof. It is the last thing my right eye sees. I watch as its trunk, its branches, and then its leaves are blotted out by the rising blood.

I am in shock. First there is intense fever, which my father tries to break using lily leaves bound around my head. Then there are chills: my mother tries to get me to eat soup. Eventually, I do not know how, my parents learn what has happened. A week after the "accident" they take me to see a doctor. "Why did you wait so long to come?" he asks, looking into my eye and shaking his head. "Eyes are sympathetic," he says. "If one is blind, the other will likely become blind too."

This comment of the doctor's terrifies me. But it is really how I look that bothers me most. Where the BB pellet struck there is a glob of whitish scar tissue, a hideous cataract, on my eye. Now when I stare at people—a favorite pastime, up to now—they will stare back. Not at the "cute" little girl, but at her scar. For six years I do not stare at anyone, because I do not raise my head.

Years later, in the throes of a mid-life crisis, I ask my mother and sister whether I changed after the "accident." "No," they say, puzzled. "What do you mean?"

15 *What do I mean?*

I am eight, and, for the first time, doing poorly in school, where I have been something of a whiz since I was four. We have just moved to the place where the "accident" occurred. We do not know any of the people around us because this is a different county. The only time I see the friends I knew is when we go back to our old church. The new school is the former state penitentiary. It is a large stone building, cold and drafty, crammed to overflowing with boisterous, ill-disciplined children. On the third floor there is a huge circular imprint of some partition that has been torn out.

"What used to be here?" I ask a sullen girl next to me on our way past it to lunch.

"The electric chair," says she.

At night I have nightmares about the electric chair, and about all the people reputedly "fried" in it. I am afraid of the school, where all the students seem to be budding criminals.

20 "What's the matter with your eye?" they ask, critically.

When I don't answer (I cannot decide whether it was an "accident" or not), they shove me, insist on a fight.

My brother, the one who created the story about the wire, comes to my rescue. But then brags so much about "protecting" me, I become sick.

After months of torture at the school, my parents decide to send me back to our old community, to my old school. I live with my grandparents and the teacher they board. But there is no room for Phoebe, my cat. By the time my grandparents decide there *is* room, and I ask for my cat, she cannot be found. Miss Yarborough, the boarding teacher, takes me under her wing, and begins to teach me to play the piano. But soon she marries an African—a "prince," she says—and is whisked away to his continent.

At my old school there is at least one teacher who loves me. She is the teacher who "knew me before I was born" and bought my first baby clothes. It is she who makes life bearable. It is her presence that finally helps me turn on the one child at the school who continually calls me "one-eyed bitch." One day I simply grab him by his coat and beat him until I am satisfied. It is my teacher who tells me my mother is ill.

25 My mother is lying in bed in the middle of the day, something I have never seen. She is in too much pain to speak. She has an abscess in her ear. I stand looking down on her, knowing that if she dies, I cannot live. She is being treated with warm oils and hot bricks held against her cheek. Finally a doctor comes. But I must go back to my grandparents' house. The weeks pass but I am hardly aware of it. All I know is that my mother might die, my father is not so jolly, my brothers still have their guns, and I am the one sent away from home.

"You did not change," they say.

Did I imagine the anguish of never looking up?

I am twelve. When relatives come to visit I hide in my room. My cousin Brenda, just my age, whose father works in the post office and whose mother is a nurse, comes to find me. "Hello," she says. And then she asks, looking at my recent school picture, which I did not want taken, and on which the "glob," as I think of it, is clearly visible, "You still can't see out of that eye?"

"No," I say, and flop back on the bed over my book.

30 That night, as I do almost every night, I abuse my eye. I rant and rave at it, in front of the mirror. I plead with it to clear up before morning. I tell it I hate and despise it. I do not pray for sight. I pray for beauty.

"You did not change," they say.

I am fourteen and baby-sitting for my brother Bill, who lives in Boston. He is my favorite brother and there is a strong bond between us. Understanding my feelings of shame and ugliness he and his wife take me to a local hospital, where the "glob" is removed by a doctor named O. Henry. There is still a small bluish crater where the scar tissue was, but the ugly white stuff is gone. Almost immediately I become a different person from the girl who does not raise her head. Or so I think. Now that I've raised my head I win the boyfriend of my dreams. Now that I've raised my head I have plenty of friends. Now that I've raised my head classwork comes from my lips as faultlessly as Easter speeches did, and I leave high school as valedictorian, most popular student, and *queen,* hardly believing my luck. Ironically, the girl who was voted most beautiful in our class (and was) was later shot twice through the chest by a male companion, using a "real" gun, while she was pregnant. But that's another story in itself. Or is it?

"You did not change," they say.

It is now thirty years since the "accident." A beautiful journalist comes to visit and to interview me. She is going to write a cover story for her magazine that focuses on my latest book. "Decide how you want to look on the cover," she says. "Glamorous, or whatever."

Never mind "glamorous," it is the "whatever" that I hear. Suddenly all I can think of is whether I will get enough sleep the night before the photography session: if I don't, my eye will be tired and wander, as blind eyes will.

At night in bed with my lover I think up reasons why I should not appear on the cover of a magazine. "My meanest critics will say I've sold out," I say. "My family will now realize I write scandalous books."

"But what's the real reason you don't want to do this?" he asks.

"Because in all probability," I say in a rush, "my eye won't be straight."

"It will be straight enough," he says. Then, "Besides, I thought you'd made your peace with that."

And I suddenly remember that I have.

I remember:

I am talking to my brother Jimmy, asking if he remembers anything unusual about the day I was shot. He does not know I consider that day the last time my father, with his sweet home remedy of cool lily leaves, chose me, and that I suffered and raged inside because of this. "Well," he says, "all I remember is standing by the side of the highway with Daddy, trying to flag down a car. A white man stopped, but when Daddy said he needed somebody to take his little girl to the doctor, he drove off."

I remember:

I am in the desert for the first time. I fall totally in love with it. I am so overwhelmed by its beauty, I confront for the first time, consciously, the meaning of the doctor's words years ago: "Eyes are sympathetic. If one is blind, the other will likely become blind too." I realize I have dashed about the world madly, looking at this, looking at that, storing up images against the fading of the light. *But I might have missed seeing the desert!* The shock of that possibility—and gratitude for over twenty-five years of sight—sends me literally to my knees. Poem after poem comes—which is perhaps how poets pray.

on sight

I am so thankful I have seen
The Desert
And the creatures in the desert
And the desert Itself.

The desert has its own moon
Which I have seen
With my own eye.

There is no flag on it.

Trees of the desert have arms
All of which are always up
That is because the moon is up
The sun is up
Also the sky
The stars
Clouds
None with flags.

If there *were* flags, I doubt
the trees would point.
Would you?

45 *But mostly, I remember this:* 45

I am twenty-seven, and my baby daughter is almost three. Since her birth I have worried about her discovery that her mother's eyes are different from other people's. Will she be embarrassed? I think. What will she say? Every day she watches a television program called "Big Blue Marble." It begins with a picture of the earth as it appears from the moon. It is bluish, a little battered-looking, but full of light, with whitish clouds swirling around it. Every time I see it I weep with love, as if it is a picture of Grandma's house. One day when I am putting Rebecca down for her nap, she suddenly focuses on my eye. Something inside me cringes, gets ready to try to protect myself. All children are cruel about physical differences, I know from experience, and that they don't always mean to be is another matter. I assume Rebecca will be the same.

But no-o-o-o. She studies my face intently as we stand, her inside and me outside her crib. She even holds my face maternally between her dimpled little hands. Then, looking every bit as serious and lawyerlike as her father, she says, as if it may just possibly have slipped my attention: "Mommy, there's a *world* in your eye." (As in, "Don't be alarmed, or do anything crazy.") And then, gently, but with great interest: "Mommy, where did you *get* that world in your eye?"

For the most part, the pain left then. (So what, if my brothers grew up to buy even more powerful pellet guns for their sons and to carry real guns themselves. So what, if a young "Morehouse man" once nearly fell off the steps of Trevor Arnett Library because he thought my eyes were blue.) Crying and laughing I ran to the bathroom, while Rebecca mumbled and sang herself off to sleep. Yes indeed, I realized, looking into the mirror. There *was* a world in my eye. And I saw that it was possible to love it: that in fact, for all it had taught me of shame and anger and inner vision, I *did* love it. Even to see it drifting out of orbit in boredom, or rolling up out of fatigue, not to mention floating back at attention in excitement (bearing witness, a friend has called it), deeply suitable to my personality, and even characteristic of me.

That night I dream I am dancing to Stevie Wonder's song "Always" (the name of the song is really "As," but I hear it as "Always"). As I dance, whirling and joyous, happier than I've ever been in my life, another bright-faced dancer joins me. We dance and kiss each other and hold each other through the night. The other dancer has obviously come through all right, as I have done. She is beautiful, whole and free. And she is also me.

Key Terms

subversive
magnolia
faze
frock
petticoat
relegated
throes
valedictorian

Questions on Meaning

1. Walker's essay addresses a common theme in our society: self image and concepts of beauty. What kinds of images of beauty are being promoted today? What effect do these images have on society?
2. Walker presents two moments from her childhood as turning points: the injury of her eye, and the day the doctor removes the "white glob" from the eye. Why are they so important to her? What changes occurred after these events?
3. Walker doesn't clearly reveal the meaning of the title until the last paragraph. What does the dance with the "other" represent?

Questions on Rhetorical Strategy and Style

1. Essays of this kind often follow an orderly step by step movement through time. Walker follows this strategy up until the accident. How does the structure seem to change after that incident? Look for how the narrator, who is in the present, interacts with the events of the past.
2. Walker's style helps us to identify and sympathize with her. Locate two or three passages you find particularly emotional. What causes that emotional response in you?
3. Walker uses the strategy of cause and effect to lend meaning to her essay and to shape it. Where is that strategy used most effectively? What things change as a result of significant events?

Writing Assignments

1. What are the dominant images of beauty in our society? Write an essay in which you, based upon those images, define beauty. Discuss what values are represented by those images and some of the problems they create. How do you feel about what those images convey?
2. Write an essay about a significant childhood event. Recount the event with enough detail so that a reader can visualize it. As Walker does, take a step by step approach in your essay and let the essay build up to the event. Also, think about the approach you might take in establishing your point of view. For example, you could write the essay as though the events were unfolding in time; or you could write it as though you were in the present moment reflecting on the past.